ISBN: 978-0-9911780-2-5

Cover Photo by Bob Peca
Cover & Book Design by Tina Fagan / www.webportfolio.com

Pissing Into the Wind

The Adventures and Misadventures
of P.J. Londo & Friends

Acknowledgments

I want to thank Debbie McCune Reynolds for her encouragement to begin this process of writing along with my wife, Judy, my daughter Angela and granddaughter Krista. Thanks also to Tina Fagan who took this project and put it into final form.

I have found in some ways that it has been good therapy and has been a cathartic experience to some extent. I hope that somehow there will be an appreciation of it if it is put in some book form. I hope that people will find an interest in my stories and appreciate some of the humor.

Introduction

My father was quite a writer even though he was poorly educated, he was extremely articulate and spent a good deal of time writing of things relating to theology. The things that were of most interest were his poems, etc. that he wrote during World War II. Unfortunately, many of these writings were lost back in the 1950's when he was teaching some kind of class. However, he had a whole volume of very interesting letters that he had written while in the South Pacific. I have a few of them left, but not many. In any event, I thought I would include one of his pieces that was written on his way back from the South Pacific in this introduction.

The last island that he was on was the small island of Tinian, where the Enola Gay took off to drop the atomic bomb on Hiroshima. Most of the people on the island did not even know what was going on, as it was highly secret and he spoke about it at some length. In any event, he wrote this poem, "Hidden Beauty".

In this poem, my father was reflecting on his three years in the South Pacific and living on the island. With some nostalgia about this little island with the native peoples and I am sure the frustrations of being stuck so far away from his family. My father hardly knew me at his time because I was born just before he left for the service in 1943. My poor mother took care of me by herself and at that time it was about $50 a month she received from his service pay. How she survived, I do not know. Unfortunately, I never really got a sense of what it was like during the war years from my parents, even though I had plenty of opportunity, time just slipped by.

E.J. Londo

Hidden Beauty

By Elton Joseph Londo

Farewell green isles of tropical enchantment, farewell oh land of whom the poets sing their praises.
Nature with beauty thee endowed if such as thee
without a soul can be called beauteous.

Or is it I who lack the soul to see? Luxuriant green
the growth that makes your land emerald, but 'neath
it all to those who seek within, a million crawling
things, the mold of death, home of pestilence.

True the windows of your heavens never shone
so bright as the inky blackness in the stillness of
your night; and in your moon is madness; what good
this madness when on must prowl the silvered coral
strands alone?

Farewell land of bandy-legged, yellow skins,
You too are in a foreign elements and lost as I.
If I beat my head on prison walls, then so do you.
Simple people, you too were made to enjoy God's
handiwork.

Living in the squalor of your germ-infested camp
Do you find beauty in this land of whom the poets

sing? Dour-visage, bland of continence, one will never know the answer; you laugh too easily, stop too abruptly, one questions its sincerity. No, deep inside I think you too long for home, hearts besting place.

Lonely isles dotting the vast watery reaches of the Pacific. Where are your rightful owners who call your bosom their birthright? Long dead these many centuries, you left the answer carved in stone unread but glowing monument to your ingenuity.

If you were to return to your home this very day you would recognize the remnants of this mortared clay and coral block/ all that remains of your lost domain?

Nature strove to mask the man-made scars, as though in anger. Weeds grow tall on stepping stones, snaking vines crawl the walls, their spreading arms covering all, even t he alter tables no longer bare.

Did you know right from wrong and still didst thou sin? Calling down the wrath of your God's to complete annulation. It must be so if you vanished, leaving neither kith nor kin.

Tell me, were you lithe and tall, dark-skinned like you Eharmorrah? If not like they per chance, more like the handsome Polynesians.

In my mind's eye I would visualize you as a su-
per-race for if he made this beauty for such as thee
Would be assuming its admirers too, be of great
grace and beauty?

Perhaps in time will bring a change, whites and
yellow departing from your 'midst, leaving you
undisputed lords of your domain.

I shall not forget you soon, returning often in reverie
And when the moon is full silvering the sand of time
From my allotted space, where I rest content, will I
come to you in spirit seeing yet again your ghostly
forms, hearing your gay laughter as you love and play,
then will I know it is the beauty of these isles, made for
you alone, of which the poets sing, not such as I.

Sail on gallant ship, clasp tight the whitened bone
between your teeth, The creaking of your booms
and masts is music to my ears. Keep that bow ever
pointed to the East, for that way lies my heart.
Kick high those heels to furthering west, this, a
prison at its best.

Farewell land of enchantment, you are a dreamer's
paradise, I too shall dream of you again, tempered
with memories of stark reality.

1942 Off to War

I recently read a book by Tom Brokaw called "The Greatest Generation", a commentary about the many people that went through the war experience and had experienced the Great Depression. They were a very hardy bunch and certainly ones, I think, had the depth that we don't see in some of the current generations.

Whatever writing skills I may possess may be a reflection of things my maternal grandfather did. He wrote extraordinary letters and I later learned that he was an illegal alien from London who had jumped ship in the early 1900's. He was very eccentric, very well educated and part of his living was selling poems that he had written. One of which had to do with Will Rogers who, at that time, was one of the most famous people in the United States. He was a very political animal who made great fun of Congress and I wish he were around these days given the political circus that is upon us. In any event my grandfather's letters were written in the old-fashioned calligraphy and they were themselves a piece of art because of his extraordinary hand writing skills that he had learned in England.

The following is a letter written to my mother in 1938

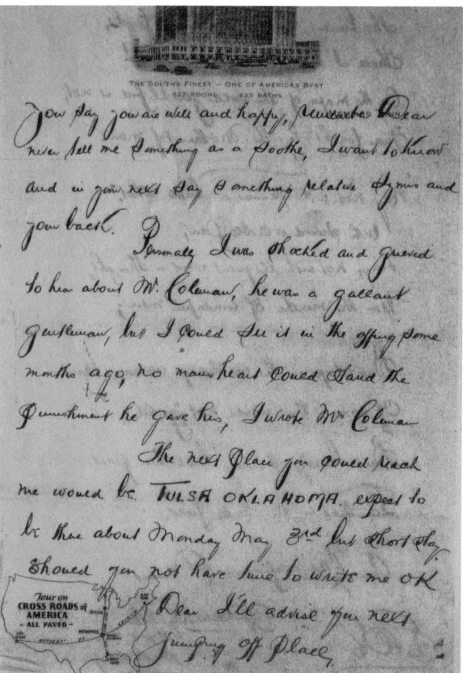

You pray you are well and happy, remember dear never tell me something as a soothe, I want to know and in your next say something relative symtoms and your back. Personally I was shocked and grieved to hear about Mr. Coleman, he was a gallant gentleman, but I could see it in the offing some months ago, no mans heart could stand the punishment he gave his, I wrote Mr Coleman

The next place you could reach me would be TULSA OKLAHOMA, expect to be there about Monday May 3rd but short stay. Should you not have time to write me OK Dear I'll advise you next jumping off place.

"The bravest battle that was ever fought,

Shall I tell you where and when?

On the maps of the world you'll find it not,

'Twas fought by the Mother of man.

"Nay, not with cannon or battle shot,

With sword or noble Pen,

Nay, not with eloquent word or thought

From the mouths of wonderful men;

But deep in the walled up woman's heart,—

Of woman that would not yield;

But bravely, silently, bore their part—

Lo, there is the battle field.

Au Revoir for now Dearest

Affectionately yrs

Daddy.

CHAPTERS

01   First Fishing and Hunting Years   1

02   The Big Woods   9

03   A Birthday to Remember – Hunting with Stevie   17

04   Musk-oxing Nunivak Bow and Arrow Style   25

05   My First Moose Ventures in Canada   43

06   Alaska Bound   55

07   Early Memorable Bear Stories in Valdez   63

08   Lake Telequana   69

09   Cousin Mike and the $50 Duck Boat   83

10   Head-Banging on the Dadina   91

11   Krista's Black Bear Hunt in Valdez   99

12   Archery Hunting for Moose in the Yukon Territory   105

13   The African Queen   115

14   Saginaw Bob and the Maple Syrup   129

15   Blood and Guts   135

16   Father-Son Caribou Adventure in the Wrangell Mountains   143

17   Oysters and Sheep Don't Mix   149

18   The Puale Bay Brown Bear Venture   161

19   The McCune Experience   171

20   The Eureka Sheep Hunt 1974   179

21   Judy the "Raffle Queen"   187

22   Of Family, Kids and Dogs   193

23   The March of the Bulls   221

24	Elk Hunting on Raspberry Island / Kodiak, Alaska	227
25	Caught With Our Pants Down	235
26	The Innoko River Fiasco	241
27	Lucky	253
28	Chronicling a Montana Goose Hunt Live	261
29	The Year of the Wolf	277
30	The Wade Clan and the Mountain Goat	287
31	The Rock Pile Elk	293
32	The Cabin on Shearwater Bay, Kodiak Island	301
33	The Wade Clan	313
34	The Kamchatka Peninsula Experience	321
35	Ironically Harry	333
36	The Birthday Buck 11/19/2017	345
37	Pops in Polar Bear Town	349
38	Sabotage in Sand Point, Alaska	353
39	The Toothless Mountain Lion	359
40	Ram Glacier	367
41	The Tale of the Linx	377
42	Mink Mania	385
43	Bulawayo or Bust	391
44	Gold in the Black Spruce	407
45	The Last Hurrah!	415

First Fishing and Hunting Years

My early days growing up were in the Minneapolis area in the suburbs, right before there were any suburbs. My earliest memories always had to do with doing things with my Dad. I was an only child and he doted on me considerably. My Dad was an avid fisherman and in those days when things were pretty frugal, fishing was a very cheap way of passing the time. I look back at old photo albums and there he was always displaying a string of fish. Some of these pictures even go back to the mid 1930's. He fished all the local lakes of Minnesota and Minneapolis, "The Land of the Lakes". He always had a fervent encentive for what he was doing. I guess that type of enthusiasm and passion was passed on to me, as I accompanied him on a number of trips, mostly just local trips and outings. In

E.J. Londo 1938

those days with no freeways, a 100-mile trip would be extraordinarily long and a really big deal.

The biggest day of the years was opening day of pheasant hunting. My Dad was very enthused with going out in spite that it was done on a very meager scale but we practiced all summer with a BB gun.

I got my first dog which was a springer spaniel, in my early years and that dog must have been very important in my upbringing because to this very day, I continue to have springer spaniels and most likely will die with one of them at my side.

I remember looking forward all year to going out bird hunting and in one day I got two birds and that was a big accomplishment I guess that sets the stage for my interest to pursue outdoor activities. I started some of my taxidermy projects, probably in my early teens even though I had no formal training, it was something that I tried to teach myself to do.

My Dad had no interest in big game hunting; in fact, he prohibited me from buying a high-powered rifle; I guess he didn't trust my judgment until I was well into my late teens.

One of my earliest experiences was with my neighborhood friend, Robert Harding, who I still maintain contact with. Back in our college days we used to hunt pheasants and ducks often with my father, but would often branch out and had our own cars to go out to western Minnesota. I still have fond memories of those hunts.

We also tried out hand at deer hunting, but we didn't

Robert Harding - My Oldest Friend and His First Deer

4

have much experience at all. I remember my first deer. I was age 19 and we were up by the McGregor area, which is about 100 miles north of Minneapolis. We accompanied on of my Dad's working friends and stayed at his cabin up there. I still remember the cold morning when that little buck came down the trail. It was a great thrill because we always dreamed of getting a deer, but never had the chance. The irony of that trip was that we were dutifully going to church, even though we were out in the country. On the way back from church, lo and behold, a much larger buck came across the road and we hit the poor bugger in the rear end. We were later able to recover it. This gentleman, who was one of my Dad's friends, never did tell the truth about the incident because I later learned that he bragged to folks that he actually bagged the deer, but didn't tell them the circumstances about it. Although, I remember vaguely about him wanting to be reimburses for the damage on his vehicle, even though at that time we were dirt broke. I think we were freshmen in college and we just didn't have the money to help fix his vehicle.

It seems like most of my life decisions have been based on my interest in pursuing some of God's creatures; both big and small.

My first job was in Duluth, Minnesota where I had a caseload in the Floodwood area which is 100 miles east of Duluth. I gained a new appreciation for deer hunting in that part of the country as it was something everybody did there. In fact, I remember all the school kids were allowed off the first week of deer season.

At that point, I took up my archery career. In those days we didn't have all the fancy equipment that they have today. The bows of today are hardly primitive equipment. There are hand-held crossbows that I think have taken away the idea of the true experience. In those days we made our own equipment, camouflage, put our own arrows together and for the most part used recurved bows. This took a lot of practice to become at all adept. The percentages of success in those days were something like less than 2% but I managed to get a deer almost every year, so that was fuel for the fire for my interest in carrying on with my archery interest.

I think the first time I ever climbed into a tree was north of Duluth. It was within an hour that a deer came by and somehow made a perfect shot on that deer, which fell right over immediately. I guess that sparked my interest to get more seriously involved in archery pursuits.

Even in the early 60's the number of deer hunters with rifles was dangerously evident. You could hardly go into the woods without taking your life in your hands. So that really inspired me to stop using rifles and also in archery season, you could be by yourself and not have the worry of the other hunters encroaching on your area so it definitely fit my lifestyle and my loner mentality.

I had a number of memorable trips over in Wisconsin, where we used to drive over the big bridge of Superior, Wisconsin. Then we went east and again it was those early experiences that seem to stick in one's memory. I think that is true of most life experiences. This was particularly true when I went to Alaska, the trips that I remember most vividly were those first ones, the novelty of it, the excitement of those times are crystal clear in my memory. The trips that have proceeded certainly seemed to have diminished in this level of consciousness.

The Big Woods

Every boy seems to have a secret place to which they can retreat to and particularly it seems for the Midwest youngster who finds solace and excitement in the woods and forests of his home area. This was the case for me as a I grew up in my early teens and beyond. We had an area across the highway and then across a very large railroad track that was called "The Big Woods". It was always an area of fascination. At the time, it was a relatively large acreage with some wooded areas and always surrounded by swamp land and some water. We spent untold times making the venture over there crossing the rather precarious highway and railroad tracks that my father always worried about to get into the woods that we spent so much time exploring.

Some of my first trapping experiences began in that area and I remember vividly the setting of traps in muskrat huts and catching a few little critters, such as weasels and muskrats. Somehow we were never able to snatch the elusive red fox that we always tried so hard to catch. But, in any event we were always excited when we did catch something and this seemed to have spawned this interest that is even with me today. All of my previous years seemed to have been fostered by these early childhood experiences.

The Big Woods was always an area that we could find retreat and there were always pheasants and ducks. We would relish in bringing my dog over there to flush pheasants and get prepared for the hunting season. I guess if you want to get a little metaphorical, the woods seemed to have been therapeutic even at that tender age and it has been with me ever since. I will always feel refreshed and renewed when I return from my little ventures in the hinderland. Thoreau referred to this in his Waldon's Pond book as the "tonic of the wilderness". Surely, there is some truth to that as I think a man needs to find that relief and the renewal by being in the quiet of the forest and being surrounded by nature's glories.

Those woods, now sadly have been demolished with the urban blight. I have returned there over the years to find it full of commercial buildings and hardly anything left but a small pond in the far east of that once immense wooded area. Interestingly, my Dad, even after I left home, would often wander over there with, mostly likely, a great deal of nostalgia and would sit quietly in the woods and ponder his son's presence. I know it was very sad when we left the area, being the only child and one he missed, I am sure. I recall when he was in the throes of his serious cancer bouts he would go over there and try to mediate and would try to encourage me to relate to what he was trying to do. Again, the therapy of being in a quiet place away from people was the beginning of my ongoing interests in the out-of-doors.

That area was also the source of problems as we became very mischievous in our teen years, to the point that we did some vandalism. The worst of it was messing with the railroad tracks that were very busy and we created some type of wheeled machine that was on the train track and this became a very serious issue. At one point we were surrounded by a number of very angry police and railroad personnel who were trying to catch the wayward teenagers that were monkeying on the railroad tracks, which caused delays in some of their schedules. So the were always looking for boys on the tracks and this was a sore point with my Dad who I found out years later had turned us into the railroad people and gave rise to our arrest. As it turned out, I don't think we spent any time in custody, but we were questioned, scorned and chastised for the dangerous situation that we had created.

In any event, this is just a little anecdote of those early days in the "The Big Woods" that I believe fostered all of my interests in getting away from the madness of humanity. Physically and mentally I always felt so refreshed when I returned from some of my hunting ventures, particularly the sheep trips, which were so arduous and it really provided a cleansing of the mind and soul. I always felt good for days after returning. Unfortunately, unless you keep up this regimen it is soon lost as you slide back into sedentary ways.

Enough said on that, I just thought it would be a good introductory comment on some of my early days that I think contributed to my fascination with the great out-of-doors.

The Wilderness

We need the tonic of wildness,
to wade sometimes in marshes where
the bittern and the meadow-hen lurk,
and hear the booming of the snipe;
to smell the whispering sedge where
only some wilder and more solitary fowl
builds her nest, and the mink crawls
with its belly close to the ground.
At the same time that we are earnest to
explore and learn all things, we require that
all things be mysterious and unexplorable,
that land and sea be infinitely wild, unsurveyed
and unfathomed by us because unfathomable.
We can never have enough of nature.
We must be refreshed by the sight of inexhaustible
vigor, vast and titanic features, the sea-
coast with its wrecks, the wilderness
with its living and its decaying trees, the
thunder cloud, and the rain which lasts
three weeks and produces freshets. We
need to witness our own limits transgressed,
and some life pasturing freely
where we never wander.

From *Walden*
by Henry David Thoreau

From Duluth, we hit the road complete with my beautiful wife, Judy, and three very small children in tow, Angela, Timothy and Patrick. I decided that I needed to advance my career so I applied to graduate school. I had several choices at the time with one being, I believe, Loyola in Chicago and the other school was the University of Manitoba in Winnipeg, Canada. The idea of getting up to the famous waterfowl areas of Manitoba helped to make my decision, for better or for worse.

So with a Volkswagen bus with no heat, Judy and I took those three children up to Winnipeg. At that time, we were surviving on $400 a month that I gained through a scholarship program that was offered by the State of Minnesota.

Winnipeg is known for its tremendous waterfowl and also for its migrations and great deer. Most of my time was consumed in my graduate school and I was only able to eke out a few weekend trips duck hunting. I also spent time trying to do some white-tailed deer hunting up in the eastern part of the providence on the Ontario border.

I did have several black bear experiences, which were my first and I was truly taken-a-back by it, by not ever having been around bears at all. This, of course, changed dramatically as we moved to Alaska where I was in an untold number of bear experiences. But, at this time, it was very exciting and I did get my first little bear, which was dumb enough to go up a tree. I brought him back with great excitement and probably tried to make him into a bear rug, this being the first of many to follow.

Timmy in Canada
First Deer

A Birthday to Remember – Hunting with Stevie

November 19. It was one of those classic days; it was one of those days when everything goes right; it was one of those rare occasions that will not soon be repeated; it was one of those days that only another duck hunter could fully appreciate.

Winter comes all too soon in our part of the world, where our brief summers slip into winter's grasp with only short reprieve, only a few golden days of autumn to temper the soul before long winter nights take hold. 1987 was no exception, Robe Lake, our favorite haunt, froze up again too soon; just when we were in the full fervor of the duck hunter's mania. The bluebills and buffleheads were on their way and so was our far too short duck hunting season. And yet, I was far from satiated from my annual pursuits.

For those not familiar with our environment, Valdez is a most idyllic coastal city in south central Alaska, on the beautiful Prince William Sound, noted for its glaciated splendor and spectacular surroundings. Often shrouded in clouds, the precipitation is typically coastal with days of eternal rain and snow accumulations of forty feet annually that would stagger the imagination of most. As the terminus of the famous Alaskan pipeline, the area gained national, if not international, notoriety but still remains a rather isolated burg. The comings and goings of the huge oil tankers poses a contradiction to our otherwise isolated and simplified lifestyles.

But true duck hunters do live here and I count myself as one of the more ardent ones, not willing to give way to our early winters and usually find a friend or two to accompany me on my extraneous ventures to the tidelands. With our favorite haunts quite inaccessible, the tidal flats off the Port of Valdez remained our sole source of late season endeavor. Many of the local mallards and geese, Lesser Canadians remain on the tidal flats most of the winter months and are safely secure by municipal ordinances restricting hunting. This is as it should be, for we can enjoy their presence daily as the main highway parallels the flats as you come into town. Some of the outskirts of the area, however, do remain open, but as any mallard hunter knows, they have come to know the boundaries all too well and comfortably spend their time in their sanctuary.

But that day was somehow meant to be special as we made our way through a foot of the year's first snowfall. Interestingly, we were not that far from the original townsite of Old Vladez, one of the original ports of entry into Alaska during the gold rush era. The town was totally devastated during the 1964 earthquake and was subsequently razed with the new town being moved to its current site approximately four miles to the west on sounder ground and safe from tidal waves they say. And so there was a lot of history not far from us as we made our way that morning. It was going to be a high tide, thirteen foot plus, which was a good indicator that it might push the birds into backwater ponds at least for a short while when the tide had crested for the day. My good friend, Stephen Goudreau scoffed as we pushed our way, having already been part of two misadventures, one of which was finding our lake frozen the previous week. The tide was coming in quickly and I was complaining as usual that we were running late, the birds would be moving and we wouldn't be ready again. We had about one-half mile to walk towards a tidal backwater that we knew would be filled and which looked ideal for the elusive greenheads. We dragged along a dozen of the now infamous "Model Perfect" Herter decoys, bluebills no less, but we figured that a decoy, even a bluebill, would be better than nothing. Bouncing through the snow with us was my constant companion of these past five years, a rarish Boykin Spaniel, a transplant from the State of Texas, a breed originally emanating from the state of South Carolina, the state dog I am told. My Boykin does not have the bravado of the Labrador or Chesapeake, but she does aim to please and braves the Alaskan waters which seldom warm above the 40 degree mark. So I don't complain, for any lack in prowess and skill she makes up in so many other ways with her temperament and congeniality.

The tidal pond was filling up quickly as we hurriedly threw our decoys in a line extending out towards the open bay, knowing that they would be difficult to retrieve and our strategy would be to wait until the tide would again recede before hopes of picking up our decoys. We settled down quickly in a makeshift blind, wrapping ourselves with a couple of old white sheets. Not particularly well disguised, it didn't seem to matter that day. Just as we settled in the wind picked up, as the winds often do from the many glacial valleys that flow into the Port of Valdez. The winds were on our backs that morning, ideal we thought to ourselves, and maybe, just maybe it would be enough to force some movement of the birds who are quite content to stay on the flats. No sooner had these thoughts passed through our heads, when a flock of mallards were on us, not hesitating, wings set, a classic confirmation that only one dreams about in retrospect. Without even murmuring so much as a whisper, both doubles were swinging and to our amazement four greenheads went splashing down in a flurry, that left us gawking to ourselves. Never does it work that way, two doubles! The usual scenario is, maybe one bird down followed by a string of invectives and accusatory remarks such as "How could you have missed?", "We might as well quit", etc.. But not this day. Our excitement of the moment was quickly projected onto the dog who was being ordered in three different directions at one time. And, in the midst of this activity we looked up to see, again to our amazement, another flock with wings set already, within range. Three more birds down, we couldn't believe it! We had hardly gathered our wits and again, the mallards appeared with little warning and with abandon, as if transfixed to decoy at any cost. Two more birds down and we were dumbfounded with our success. The birds began to pile up in the snow and we felt like small boys at Christmastime, greedily stacking our booty. Within an hour eleven birds were down, almost all drakes and with only one bird lost, one that had dove on us as they often do. We looked for a long time that morning for that

Myself and Stephen Goudreau
A Banner Day at the Site of Old Valdez Township

bird hoping that somehow such perfection would not be marred, our consolation knowing that some vigilant eagle would have a change in menu that day.

Many pictures were taken that morning knowing that such a spectacle may not soon be repeated and certainly we wanted to capture the moment.

We stashed the decoys with thoughts of trying to come back again before the season closed, secretly knowing that we would not ever be able to replicate the excitement of that morning, but just in case.

A makeshift knapsack from our sheets bundled up the birds as we made our way home, with a sense of satisfaction that we were excited to share with a few of our cronies who we knew would appreciate our experience. A little bragging was in order. On the way back to town both of my mink sets, the first of the year held fur, but what else would I have expected, a bonus for sure, of fowl and fur, icing on the cake one could say, for it was my birthday – that day, that perfect day when everything went the way it should go, when the wind was going in the right direction and the decoys dancing as if orchestrated and the birds responding as if choreographed and even the players that day seemed to have an uncanny rhythm to their skill. Truly a birthday to remember!

This story was published in "Alaska Magazine".

Musk-oxing Nunivak – Bow and Arrow Style

Frustratingly sitting at Mile 19 of the Richardson High-way our long-awaited adventure had all the earmarks of another fiasco. It was February 19th and the third day that Thompson Pass had been closed and there was some question as to whether it would be open today. Our plane to Bethel was to have left Anchorage at 7 pm Sunday and here we were at 2:30 in the afternoon with three hundred miles to go. Larry and I both resigned ourselves to the fact that we were not going to make our plane connection but hoped that we could make it out the following day. Although having lived and hunted in Alaska for the past five years it is still difficult to accept those conditions which are out of my control. However, in Alaska, one soon realizes that the weather dictates everything and that the success or failure of a hunt is very closely contingent on the whims of Mother Nature. This is particularly true in our city of Valdez and in particular the fall and winter of 1976-1977 where the flying conditions had been impossible and the road over Thompson Pass not much better. But here we were on another adventure and a very expensive one at that. Larry Dunny and myself were employees of the Harborview Developmental Center, a State facility for the intellectually disabled and it was Larry's brainstorm to make application for the spring 1977 musk-ox hunt. This was only the third year that the hunt had been open, the first being in the fall of 1975. Forty-five permits were to be issued this year but as with most drawings, we didn't feel we had a chance to draw a permit, let alone two. The reality of the fact that we could make such a hunt took awhile to absorb, particularly when we had to reflect over our savings accounts and credit references. Despite the pipeline impact, Valdez is still small enough in which one gets to know his friendly banker in a small-town kind of way. The permit alone for the resident was $500 which is somewhat mind-boggling. The only rationalization being the uniqueness of the hunt and the hoped for one-in-a-lifetime experience. There is but one wild musk-ox herd in Alaska located on Nunivak Island, and it has never been open to sport hunting until the fall of 1975. The hunt was precipitated by the excessive number of large bulls, who were not longer contributing to the healthy growth of the animals on the island. The hopes for a trophy sized animal were greatly enhanced by these factors.

It was 3:00 pm when over the CB radio came the good news that an escorted convoy was being taken over the pass. So with a renewed surge of enthusiasm, off we were to Anchorage. Monday morning found us dragging our usual voluminous amounts of gear into the International Airport. You somehow tend to forget the irritations and anxieties of waiting in busy airports but once again, we found ourselves standing in line with duffel bags, packs and gun cases. Going through security is always an amusing and at times embarrassing experience. One forgets how many pockets, nooks and crannies there are in your many layers of down clothing and cold weather gear. Extricating from every possible crevasse comes bullets, compasses, knives, etc., to the point where the impatient security lady pulls you aside and delicately probes for any violations. The incongruousness of jet aircraft an wilderness Alaska come face to face in these kinds of situations and is reflective of the changing character of our "last frontier". Our reservations somehow had been cancelled we were advised and we found ourselves on the stand-by list. Despite my pessimistic grumbling our names were finally called and we were boarded and on our way to Bethel.

There, we met our guide, Jobe Weston who had agreed to take us out on the island. Jobe had grown up on the island but due to the lack of employment opportunities he moved to Bethel and was currently working for the Alaska Legal Services. He advised us that we would be leaving for Mekoryuk the following morning and that he had been successful in finding village people to escort us via snow machine across to the southwest side of the island where the animals wintered. We decided to charter one of the local air services for the purpose of gaining a better perspective of the island and an approximate location of the animals. Our Cessna 206 taxies smoothly across the frozen Kuskokwim River then into a foggy morning sunshine. Visibility was poor for the first fifteen to twenty minutes but soon we broke into blue skies, which is always a comforting relief for anyone who flies in bush Alaska. Soon we were over Bering Sea heading towards Nelson and Nunivak Island. Below us lie the myriad of geometric configurations formed by the ever-changing ice pack. One is immediately struck by the bleakness and awesome nothingness of the tundra and terrain. This feeling persisted throughout the trip and was much more real as we found ourselves bouncing along the unmeasured whiteness of Nunivak. As we approached the island we skirted the southwest shore and spotted a number of groups of animals. The first group that we spotted were close to the village and we were impressed with the first sighting of musk-ox in the wild. There were four bulls clustered together on a snowy ridge of which one was a very impressive animal. As we came by them, they huddled shoulder to shoulder and swung their heads from side to side. We were encouraged; but in my mind, I questioned how we would ever located the animals in such trackless space.

As we approached the Mekoryuk air strip, which was nothing but a flat bit of tundra near the village, our pilot pointed out a downed aircraft who he said was owned by a friend of his who had miscalculated during bad weather. He glibly reported that is what happened to the last musk-ox hunters that ventured forth on Nunivak. With the lack of landmarks and the intensity of the whiteness I could see how easy it would be to lose one's sense of direction. The "air terminal" comprised of a small wooden shack, which apparently house the hand pushed snowblower. We were advised that it had not been operable for a number of days and that new snow would mean closure of the run-way to wheeled aircraft. This was a comforting thought as we saw our plane lift into blue skies and quickly go out of sight. Snow machines and sleds soon appeared, gear was loaded and off we were, skimming across the now to the village which was approximately a mile away. I don't know how to adequately describe Mekoryuk but it is like, I'm sure, many Alaskan villages, a clustering of unpainted dwellings surrounded by a sea of snow and ice. The population is somewhere around one hundred during the winter. Strange little street signs stick our seemingly to direct some unknown traffic, although the only vehicles in Mekoryuk during the winter are snow machines which dart and in and out of the wind swept abodes.

We were warmly greeted by Jobe's parents, Mr. and Mrs. Henry Weston, who were obviously a different generation Eskimo family. Although they language was a barrier we managed to convey our feelings through a series of smiles and gestures. We also met Milt and Beverly Stevens, who were to accompany us on our hunt. Milt and Beverly were from Anchorage and both had hunted extensively in Alaska and had equally been intrigued with the promise of a hunt for musk-ox. They too had both drawn permits, which led us to discuss the actually number of applications submitted. We later learned that there were approximately one hundred, which either indicated that the hunt had not been widely publicized or the expense involved had discouraged would-be nimrods.

The day was a very beautiful and clear and one and all were anxious to take advantage of this good luck knowing that the weather could change very rapidly. As Jobe advised and as we could easily envision.

The winds on the island could easily delay the hunt for days; for even the villagers who have lived on the island all their life will not venture forth when blizzard conditions prevail. Even on a clear day it would not be well advised to venture into such country without someone who was familiar with the area. Jobe advised us that we would have to wait until the following morning because he was having difficulty locating a replacement snow machine and escort. That day and evening was spent chatting and for the most part exchanging hunting stories and adventures. We were served very excellent "Gussick" food whereas Mr. Weston preferred his more traditional foods and would quietly go off by himself to cut frozen pieces of reindeer with his ulu, dipping them into seal oil with gusto and a smile. He generously offered to share but had not takers. There is a substantial reindeer herd on the island and most of the meat for the islanders is derived from this, however, it is seal, walrus and fish in the summer that constitutes the remaining bulk of their diet.

That night the winds picked up and thoughts of a delayed hunt flashed through our minds as we tried to sleep. The winds had quieted by morning and we were hopeful that we could be on our way. There was a scurry of activity as snow machines and sleds were gathered and as gear was loaded and covered with canvas; a curious throng of villagers gathered. My Jennings Compound bow seemed to prick the curiosity of some, particularly of Mr. Weston, who picked it up and mockingly stalked an imaginary beast. He laughed and posed for pictures and I wondered how many decades had gone by since the Native Alaskans had used such archaic weaponry. Amidst the excitement was a solemn moment in which a number of the elders prayed quietly in a circle and feeling ignorantly ill at ease, we were advised that one of the villagers had died the previous evening and this was a prayer for him. In any events, the gathering before the hunt seemed reminiscent of what I could envision as traditional preparations that probably were part of the village culture for countless ages. The Stevens' were cozily tucked away in a large freighter sled amidst caribou hides and white canvas and if it were not for the mechanical dog that pulled it, it could have been a scene out of Dr. Zhivago. Accompanying us besides Jobe were three of the villagers, two of which were elders, namely Jack Williams and Ben Whitman, both I understand in their sixties but looking to be a very sinewy forty-five. Complete with mukluks and seal gloves, it was indeed an added touch to the aesthetics of the expedition. The fourth member was Moses John, we was a younger fellow but had a very enthusiastic, warm small and very proudly told me that he had managed to keep his machine going for six years. With the directive of Mr. Williams, the machines were started and with great anticipation we were off to the interior of the island. I sat precariously perched on a sled filled with gas cans and miscellaneous gear and Larry equally was holding on for dear life as we went bounding through the trackless wastelands. What is strangely interesting is that there is nary a tree or a bush to be seen, mostly flatness with occasional slow rising hills and dips. At times there were river bottoms to cross, however, it was difficult to distinguish the terrain. Our goal was to move to the southwest part of the island where we could make camp at one of the summer fish camps. For the most part these consisted of sod huts that were dug into the side of the hills, although there were a few wooden structures that would provide temporary quarters. The weather improved as the day went on and as we headed towards the end of the island, the snow conditions also improved. Our sleds were extremely heavy and soft and drifted snow posed difficulties at times. Keeping the momentum going was the secret of not getting bogged down, however, on long inclines it was often necessary to desled and push by hand.

Our first attempts were to locate the four animals that we had seen the previous day. However, we were unable to locate them and after a number of hours of searching, it was decided that our best chance would be to set up a base camp where there would be access to a number of animals which would be better opportunity for the four hunters. We finally arrived at what Jack Williams smilingly referred to as his "hotel", which was his sod house that he used during fishing season. We opted however to continue down the coast into an area which we thought would put us closer to the herds that we had seen. As we went we sighted three bulls that looked promising but the day was quickly coming to a close and we felt we should make camp before it became too late. These strange beasts stood by the hillside looking curiously as us. One's first impression upon seeing a musk-ox in the wild is that is most definitely must have some prehistoric origins. There is an almost grotesque quality to its shaggy form and with the steam and frost vaporizing from its head, it is indeed an eerie sight.

Arriving at the other fish camp we busily dug down to where we could enter into the hut and made whatever other provisions we had to for the night. In the meantime the remaining group went off to do some preliminary explorations of the coastline. Larry had accompanied the group and they were successful in spotting a large number of animals late in the evening. They returned to camp by the lights of their machines to report that it looked very promising indeed for the following morning. They had excited tales of being charged by an old bull with a broken horn, forcing them to make a very quick exodus. Milt embarrassingly reported that there were at least ten foot spaces between his tracks and he finally found himself tumbling down the hill with camera and all. Larry had found a very acceptable animal and had taken his shot but because of the darkness, could not recover the animal until the following morning.

The sod hut was a very cozy scene with Ben having managed to warm the cold interior with a fire of driftwood that had been left there from the previous summer. A group of us tented outside and did not have the good fortune to have heard the old tales and myths that were told by Jack and Ben regarding the beginnings of the island and all of the ancestry that followed.

The night passed with visions of musk-ox running through our heads only to be dispelled by the morning's chilly awakening. Emerging from a warm sleeping bag has always been the most painful experience of winter camping but today it was easier with the promise of a clear, quiet day and with musk-ox a short distance away. Moses had not brought a sleeping bag and he had remarked that one or two nights out is not too bad and that he had done this many times before by just crawling into a snow bank. The temperatures had been somewhere in the teens although and I'm sure that night it was close to zero. The Stevens' however, had an extra sleeping bag so fortunately Moses did not have to prove his prowess which as least made me feel more comfortable.

The herd of approximately thirty animals were easily located and they were situated on top of a group of sand dunes, which stretched along the beach area. This allowed for excellent stalking, as there were enough ridges and gulleys that provided good cover. This was better than was expected, in that I had thought they would be in completely wide open country, which would have made stalking more difficult. The herd formed in their traditional phalanx, the bulls shoulder to shoulder, with their heads down, the cows and calves huddles behind. Approaching the animals was not a problem as we had heard and the biggest difficulty was locating a bull that would offer a good shot. With the close clustering of the animals it was difficult to locate a large animal from a small one and we were advised to look closely at the formation of the horns. The larger the base of the horn and the less hair between the horns, the bigger the animal. Mrs. Stevens was first to score, picking out a large bull and downing it with one shot. Shortly after that we were able to recover Larry's animal who had separated from the herd and had been making its way out towards the ocean. It died on the icepack, luckily not going too far from shore which could have been a problem in recovery. The herd separated into a number of smaller herds and moved down the coast along the dune area. Milt Stevens was the next one to take an animal chose an equally excellent bull.

The next several hours were spent skinning and butchering the animals, with the help of our guides. It was only when one got into the actual skinning that you realized how thick the hide and long and luxurious the hair was. They were indeed a very unique animal.

With the hopes of taking a musk-ox with my bow, I had been encouraged by the fact that they were easily approached and with no wind and the sand dune area, it looked like a close shot could be made. However, my concern was the thickness of the hide and the hair, which would make it very difficult for adequate penetration. I had in fact experimented with Larry's animal and disappointingly found that the arrow had poor penetration. The musk-ox seem to be three-quarters shoulder and with his hump and brisket and massive shoulder muscles, the best shot would have to be an angling one into the vital areas. IT was with mixed optimism that we proceeded down the coast looking for the herd, particularly the one large bull that seemed to have been leading the group. Several miles down from Milton's kill, we came upon five animals and the approach began. Accompanied by Jobe and with Jack and Larry looking on with camera in hand, we moved up the hill to where the animals were standing. They were ideally sitting in a small pocket and we could move up quite close to them. The noticeably larger animal was a good bull and he was standing broadside as we rounded a ridge. I nervously moved my sight down to 50 yards and let fly. The first arrow was true but sailed over the animal's back. The next shot was held lower and was well placed in the center of the shoulder but not far enough back actually, I thought, for good penetration. The animal seemed to shudder a bit but did not seem particularly disturbed. The third shot was also high as the animals began to mill around, but with this the bull turned offering a shot at his other flank. Another good shot was placed but again, I was not happy with penetration. The animal stood there with arrows protruding from both sides reminiscent of a Madrid bullfight as my fifth and last arrow disappeared underneath his hairy brisket. I was mad at myself for shooting too quickly on the last shot, realizing after that I could have approached the animal much closer and could have made a killing shot. So there I stood somewhat frantic with no arrows and only left with the hope that the old bull would lay down and die. I was encouraged by the fact that he appeared to be weakening and was less steady on his feet. Also, he made no attempt to follow the other animals, which were now making their way down a hill and up the coastal ridges. The bull then made an attempt to follow but losing its footing tumbled down a steep hill, only to get up on its feet again and begin walking towards the ocean shore. I followed quickly and happened upon one of the arrows that I had missed with, unusual luck

Nunivak Eskimo Guides

considering the snow conditions. This I placed behind the shoulder with no apparent effect. The bull continued to walk, lying down frequently, as if wanting to sleep, and my optimism grew. Finally as if oozed out of life, he lay down and did not get up again. I was left with a rather mixed triumphant feeling; however, despite what our anti-hunting friends might say, the killing of an animal is always anticlimactic and while the kill is an essential part of the hunt, it is certainly by no means, all of what hunting is about.

It was 2:30 pm and we had much work ahead of us if we were to return to Mekoryuk that day. However, the weather conditions continued to be good and there was an implicit message that we should take advantage of it. We hurriedly skinned and boned out the animal, sleds were loaded and we began to make our return to the village. We were fortunate that the snow conditions were good, in that the sleds were extremely heavy and the machines would have had extreme difficulties if the snow had been soft and drifted. We arrived in Mekoryuk in darkness with tenderly sore behinds from the many hours of strained sitting.

As fortune would have it, the weather conditions quickly deteriorated and by morning, the winds were blowing at thirty to forty knots. The hunt may have had a different outcome had we delayed. We were advised that the Mekoryuk airfield was closed to wheeled aircraft and we

Margaret Faverty, Teacher
Musk-ox Presentation

had to radio for a charter on skis. Hurried goodbyes and thank yous were made as we loaded musk-ox and gear into the 185. We were accompanied by a village lady who was on her way to Bethel to have a baby and so we found ourselves jammed among gear and musk-ox hides. As we headed for Bethel I reflected on the question that Moses Johns has innocently posed earlier in the trip, "Why would you want to shoot a musk-ox?", and as I recalled I had some difficulty in explaining what the motivation was.

Preliminary scoring of all the animals placed them into the Boone and Crockett category, with scores over one hundred. Ninety points is the minimum to place in the scoring. Mine was only the third ever taken by means of bow and arrow and I stand a chance of placing quite high in the book.

Submitted to "Alaska Magazine" 1980.

My First Moose Ventures in Canada

While in Winnipeg attending graduate school at the University of Manitoba I met a number of interesting folks. One of which whose name was Gerhard Suss, a first generation German whose father had fought on the German side of World War II. Gerhard was an extremely bright fellow and I recall he had a vocabulary that was humbling. He had an arrogance about him that made him stand out and I was taken with his willingness to do some adventuresome activities. He has previously been working for the probation department and had lived in some of the far north communities of Manitoba; i.e.: Flin Flon and the Pas area. So had some experience navigating the waters of Manitoba, which are immense given the geography. Gerhard and I did have a number of trips that I felt would be worth repeating in some form. At the time we were so young and dumb that we didn't know well enough how dangerous situations could develop as is with most young people. I believe at the time I was age 25. One particular narrow escape from death was an ill-advised trip across the narrows of Lake Winnipeg. Lake Winnipeg is a huge, almost ocean size lake and there is a narrow spot that is approximately 2-5 miles across and Gerhard had the brainstorm to go fishing on the Bloodvein River which is on the opposite side of the lake. We ventured across this water with a 17-foot canoe and a very tiny little outboard motor. As I recall the trip across went relatively smooth and then we spent a day or two fishing the Bloodvein River catching Walleyed Pike.

The return trip however was a different story and we found ourselves in the middle of this huge lake with crosswinds that were putting us at great risk. I remember laying flat on the bottom of the canoe as the waves were splashing over the sides of the canoe and if it had gone over we would have had no recourse, as we would have been blown into oblivion. I remember that the crossing seemed to be forever and we had no clue at what kind of risk that we had put ourselves into. That indeed would have been an early demise to two careers but in retrospect one just ponders those outcomes and passes it off as just one of the poor decisions that one makes in their youth.

It was during this time that we had made several unsuccessful forays trying to take down a Manitoba moose. This is something that was high on our list and we always had great expectations but never were successful. One particular situation at the time was extremely aggravating as a good friend of ours from Duluth, Minnesota namely John Hayden had accompanied us on a trip again with the use of canoes down a very long stretch of river into an extensive bog area. It was during that time that John had wounded a bull moose and for whatever the reason failed to follow up and recover the animal out of nervousness or whatever caused him not pursue it in a timely way. By the time we had returned to where he was, the moose, I could still see in my mind's eye was making it's way across this huge bog area and it was obviously crippled and we were never able to recover the animal. This was indeed a great source of sadness as losing an animal of that size is difficult to swallow. At that time it was particularly important as we had made so many other efforts to find a moose and now we found ourselves in another ugly situation.

After graduation from the University of Manitoba I entered into the one of the more bizarre trips of my youth. I returned to Manitoba in the fall of 1969 probably not very legally as I did not have any visa status remaining and technically was a non-resident alien that would require a guide to do any hunting. Somehow I had found an air taxi service in north central Manitoba that we made arrangements with for a fly-in trip, the first of our careers. The trip involved several hundred miles of driving and then we took a railroad spur that went into an abandoned gold mining town of Sherridon, Manitoba. There is quite a history to this little town and there was a lot of very interesting old buildings remaining, one of which was the local hotel, that we stayed at. This subsequently had burned not that many years ago in 2012 and I believe many of the remaining buildings were transported to a different community. In any event we started our trip from this location and flew off of a small lake on a floatplane probably a 185 Cessna. This trip turned out to be checkered with more than a few miscues because of our total lack of experience to do anything that we undertook. The trip seemed to get more bizarre as the days went on and I did not even know the name of the lake that we were dropped off at but we made arrangements of course for a pickup a week later. We had a canoe strapped onto the pontoons, which is now not legal and had very skimpy gear and I remember a very inadequate tent. As it turned out we landed on this unnamed lake and it was on the far end away from the river tributary that flowed out and one that we ended up spending a good deal of time exploring. The tributary was were we spent the most of our hunting efforts. Our hunting weapons comprised of two military style old bolt action rifles with iron sights and not much more. I believe that the particular gun I had was an old Mauser action newly remodeled from Sears for the grand total price of $39. I also had dragged along my trusty little bow and arrow with hopes of somehow impaling a moose.

From the onset the weather was deplorable and it seemed to be raining almost continuously and we spent most of our time wet or damp. Each day for a number of days we made the relatively long ride down the lake to the river where we floated looking and trying to get some handle on how to hunt the wily moose. However I think somewhere in the early parts of the trip the outboard motor gave up the ghost and we found ourselves paddling the entire length of the lake more than a few times at which point we decided that maybe we should change our camp to the far end of the lake and closer to the river. We found a rather classic old trapping cabin that was moss covered but a far better shelter than our leaking tent. It was during this time that I shot a lynx from the boat which was quite a feat given the lack of stability in the canoe and it was the first one I had ever seen and I remember that I was elated that I had taken such an elusive critter.

1969 Trapper Cabin and Lynx

At some point in the later part of the week we had heard some moose activity as it was during the rutting season and we were encouraged that maybe we would have some success. I believe it was the last day of the hunting time that we found ourselves looking at three different moose that were along the river's edge and with a volley of shots two of them were on the ground, one in the river and the other one on the shoreline. We were boggled by our great fortune and we had literally used up all of the ammunition that we had. The next couple days were an absolute fiasco of incompetence that I still shake my head at. The one rather bizarre anecdote was that the bull moose was still alive when we approached it and we were out of bullets and I found myself sinking an arrow into the critter and I was so adrenaline charged I actually ran up the animal and pushed the arrow further into his vitals. This obviously was not a very smart move given the flailing legs and head. Now we were faced with the prospect of what to do with these two gigantic animals having no experience with how to quarter them and or skin them properly. The first obstacle was to try to find a way to remove the one that was in the water and we found ourselves into the night with a lantern to try to extricate it from the water with the use of a very tiny rope wench. This seemed to take almost half of the night then we started to dismember the critter in some fashion. All I remember is that we spent the entire night with the aid of a lantern trying to quarter these critters and then placing them in the canoe and then carefully paddling in the dark across the lake to our abode. I have one picture of the canoe that was literally filled to the brim with huge quarters of moose meat and again the naiveté of paddling with that amount of weight could have been disastrous particularly in the night where we didn't have a real handle on where we were going. Somehow we managed to bring back both animals some of which still had the hide on and the horns and head were still attached to the bull. It was a grand pile of moose that we did not have a clue of what to do from that point forward. It seems that a day or so later our pilot circled over and landed and proceeded to berate us with a great degree of anger for sure on what situation he had got into because of our ignorance. He had no clue that we had left the previous campsite and was worried that something disastrous had happened to us and has spent a great deal of time looking for us. The consternation by the pilot was more than a little visible as he saw this huge pile of moose meat that was poorly handled and the difficulties of hauling these huge pieces of moose in his small aircraft became a dilemma. The entire moose head and neck were still intact and he told us there was no way for that to be taken unless we would dissect it further. So somehow we managed to whittle the neck and at some point he was able to wrangle the head into the airplane. I can't remember but I'm sure it took several trips to do so. When we finally arrived back in the little town of Sherridon we had the next ordeal to figure out ways to load this thousand pounds of meat, etc. onto empty boxcars. This in itself is quite a feat as the boxcars are at least six feet high and we had to lift and struggle with each piece to get them up but our youth and determination prevailed. Following this we made our way back to the old hotel and I as remember we started drinking some good Canadian beer to the point where the train was about to leave and the owner yelled at us that if we didn't get down there we were going to be left for another week as the train only made its way off this short spur on a weekly basis. So again this trip was one crazy mistake of youth and inexperience that made it memorable.

The next obstacle that we really hadn't given much serious thought to was how we were going to transport at least one of the moose over and through customs. As previously noted, I did not have a license and or provisions for being a non-resident alien and we were scratching our heads about what to do. Somehow Gerhard had in his knowledgebase some old gravel road that crossed into the United States that was not supervised by Customs. So we transported the whole critter with antlers and all on this abandoned road. This surely would not fly in today's concerns with security and we would probably be in major difficulties with the legal system.

I remember that my wife Judy and our three kids who were indeed very small at the time somehow had driven our little Volkswagen bus from Minneapolis to this prearranged point and God knows how she found her way. It's a

My First Moose

little unclear as to how I got to Winnipeg in the first place whether I took a train or I don't know because we only had one vehicle. In any event we successfully subverted the system and with a vehicle full of horns, antlers and moose meat with the three kids we found our way back to our rental in Anoka, Minnesota. I recall bringing the head over to one of the local taxidermist and he said it was beyond repair given the time it had been left unattended.

Nonetheless I took it on as my first taxidermy project and began to build a form from scratch using chicken wire, two by fours, etc. trying to reconstruct a form-like head for this beast. I didn't have the skinning skills but somehow managed to put it together. In lieu of a standard tanning process I used a pickling solution, which had been used for centuries. The end product gets the hide extremely hard so one has to work with it while it is still wet. In any event that moose head stood in that little apartment basement for a number of years and then made it's way over to my father's garage where it stayed for God knows how many years and finally at some point I cut off the antlers and they are currently in my son's home in the Springfield, Massachusetts area. If those horns could talk they surely had a good one to tell as it was transported as noted to a number of places and I forgot that it actually went to Alaska for awhile then subsequently shipped to my son where his kids designed some ornate plaque identifying the year that it was taken, etc.

This adventure certainly personified the level of incompetency that we possessed at that time and I often flash back on our ignorance but it was those early ventures that seem to stick with you. Gerhard went on to be a very successful administrator in the Manitoba Department of Corrections for many years. In recent years I tried to get in touch with him and found out that he in fact, he was living in China and teaching and we did have some correspondence but not many years after that I found out through his son who lives in Winnipeg that he recently passed away. So unfortunately we were unable to reminisce about the craziness of those times. I spent some time putting together a letter for his son and found a few pictures that I sent along to him that highlighted some of the adventures that I had undertaken with his father.

Alaska Bound

Following my return from graduate school I was obligated to spend three years in Minnesota as part of the repay for funds that I received during my graduate school. During those few years I was able to squeeze in some weekend trips mostly over to Wisconsin for some deer hunting and archery ventures. It was during that time that I worked at the Anoka State Hospital a rather bleak place built God knows probably at the turn of the century and it personified the harshness of the state mental hospitals of the time. We worked on the adolescent unit which was quite a challenge however I learned a good deal of behavioral techniques and I would liked to think that maybe we did provide some helpful experience for the clientele that resided there. Given the austere physical environment it made it very difficult to provide a very therapeutic milieu but we tried our best and at that time I was fresh out of graduate school and had been operating out of a good deal of idealism and optimism that I could help in making some changes with the young people involved.

In the meantime my kids of course were growing and the oldest, Angela, was attending one of the local grade school and I began to ponder our future. I accepted a position at the St. Joseph's Children Home in south Minneapolis and those arduous days of driving through the freeways and traffic probably contributed to my think-

1973 - Early Days in Valdez

Robe Lake in Valdez

ing that I didn't really want to do this kind of thing the rest of my life. Somehow I concluded that Alaska was the place to be and I'm sure I did considerable reading and this inspired me to submit some applications to the state of Alaska. It took several years of the application process before a job offer occurred and I was later told that one of the most major air disasters in Juneau where all were lost and probably had my application aboard on it's way to the central office. This not being known, I resurrected another application and several job offers materialized and then it was time for the big decision. I know my parents were emotionally crushed with the prospects of us leaving Minnesota as these were their only grandchildren and my father in particular was extremely distraught with this decision. I'm sure this was a reflection of the fact that he never really had much of a family in his growing up years and he was enthralled with his grandchildren and now to see them leaving was more than he could manage. I often wonder how much of this contributed to the early onset of cancer that took his life in 1980. However he had struggled with the disease for several years prior to that and I often thought that maybe the stresses of lonesomeness, etc. could have been a contributing factor but that's just my conjecture at this stage of the game. It is interesting to note that my dad had entertained thoughts of going to Alaska when he was in the Service as there was a program offering homesteads to people in the Palmer, Alaska area just outside of Anchorage and it seduced a good deal of farmers from Iowa and Minnesota up to that area and they developed it remarkably into a pretty substantial farming area. They were called "settlers" and some of them still retain property to this day. However most of this property comprises the Matanuska Valley which is now the bedroom community for Anchorage and many subdivisions have grown up and now they're many folks every day that commute to Anchorage as they escape the growing Anchorage urban area to find some solitude out in the more rural local. It seems that my father was very content to remain in Minneapolis and his travel days were essentially over when he returned from the war. Three years of living in terrible conditions really took it's toll in terms of his interest in making long ventures. He did make one trip with a new vehicle for us in the late 70's and then took his first airplane trip with my mother.

As noted I received several job applications interests, one being in Ketchikan in southeast Alaska and the other from Valdez, which had just suffered the catastrophic destruction of the "old town" in 1964 earthquake. The new town was relocated to approximately four miles away and was rebuilt on more solid ground. It just so happened that the first governor of Alaska was a gentleman name Bill Egan and he, with much controversy, decided he needed to do something to salvage the economy of Valdez so he contrived to open up a mental health facility also with a medical component given that there were no such facilities at that time. This became one of the primary employment sites as the earthquake took their shipping industry and there was not much left except for the State of Alaska

Highway Department and what was to become the Harborview Memorial Hospital that was built in 1967. There was some meager commercial fishing but certainly not a very sustainable economy for those that remained. I believe when we arrived in 1972 there were only 700 people in this town.

My second effort at reapplying for a job in Alaska materialized and following a phone call from the superintendent from the facility that hired me we and made plans to head north. This was in August of 1972. This was during the pre-Alaska pipeline days and Valdez at the time was a very humble city still reeling from the earthquake of '64 and all the moves to the new town site. It consisted primarily of trailers and a few homes and businesses that were physically transported from the "old town". We found ourselves living in what they called state housing, a three-bedroom apartment that we were lucky to have given the availability of housing, which was essentially nonexistent. Conditions were quite simple to say the least, as there was no television and the only radio station was the armed forces station and a small newspaper put out by the Day family who at that time ran a number of businesses in town including insurance and a clothing store. The Day family in itself is quite a story as they had originally settled across the bay in what was called Dayville and that property was sold to the Alyeska pipeline people for some extraordinary money and became the hub of all of the oil activity that has occurred during the last 40 years. Judy became very acquainted with Mrs. Day and actually went to work for her at the clothing store very soon after our arrival.

The level of activity related to the pipeline had not yet begun although the pipe was stacked in huge rows out approximately four miles from town awaiting all of the various environmental approvals. During that delay the pipe became corrosive and the first real labor activity involved cleaning the pipes which provided some great employment opportunities for the early workers. This was just the tip of the iceberg for the 10,000 workers that descended on the city within a few years. I took a position at the Harborview Memorial Hospital and our salaries at the time were indeed humble compared to what the oil related jobs where offering. At the time there were few employment options namely the hospital and the department of transportation. Other than that there was a few gift stores, bars and restaurants but that was about all. When we arrived in Alaska we of course were overwhelmed by the completely different environment that we had been accustomed to in our earlier years. Interestingly, we ran into quite a few people from Minnesota and as it turned out our whole block was comprised of people that lived in various parts of Minnesota. The other group that we became very familiar with was a group from Michigan and we soon found ourselves with a very compatible group of people of similar age and interests. Many of these friendships have been sustained throughout the years and are sadly missed at this time. Many of the people that I have met in those early days were people that I made the various trips around the state in which I will try to provide some storyline to these adventures.

Early Memorable Bear Stories in Valdez

One of the first experiences that I had shortly following my arrival to Valdez was my preoccupation with the bears in the area. This was all new and exciting as my previous experiences had very little to do with bears as we grew up as noted in the Midwest. Valdez at that time had only 700 people and as noted previously it had little development. My first effort at chasing the wily black bear was down the coast on the flats in the Mineral Creek area and at that time there was no development except for one small little cabin. It was a very pretty area surrounded of course by mountains and a labyrinth of creeks that flowed into the ocean. In September the creeks were still full of salmon and I fumbled my way through this maze of tangled swampland and learned very early about the tidal movements and how it affected the depths of the various creeks. My first trip down to the Mineral Creek flats was on the opening day of the season, which was September 1, 1973. I took my beat up old aluminum canoe and I'm not sure if I motored down or paddled down several miles to the creek area and was planning to spend the weekend down in there in hopes of seeing a bear. As it turned out I got more than I bargained for as I was naively walking from one salmon stream to another really not prepared for what I had to do deal with it at the time. I had carried my archery equipment with me and was sitting the first evening on the creek bottom and low and behold a bear made his appearance and as I was about to let an arrow fly, I found myself a bit panicky about what I was about to do and grabbed my old .30-06 rifle and proceeded to knock the poor critter down. I was astonished that I had accomplished this in such a short order and as the night approached I still had not recovered the bear although it was a relatively short distance away. As the darkness grew and I was looking for this particular bear up jumped a much larger bear standing on his hind legs and scared the hell out of me. I instinctively let a shot go out in plain desperation and panic. And this bear also went down and into the darkness. At that point I was beside myself with what to do and now I had a fair degree of fear as I thought I was surrounded by wounded bears and didn't have a clue what to do. Fortunately I made my way to the cabin that was not that far and sat there most of the night awake and pondering what I had done and the situation that I had created. As I sat through the night in the darkness I could hear other bears splashing and my God I thought I was in bear heaven and didn't know what to make of it all.

As daylight came I saw more bears and was still able to wander around to where I had been and was successful in finding both of the bears deceased. I then was faced with the dilemma with how to retrieve them bearing in mind that I only had the canoe to get back to the town as at the time there were no roads and it would have been extremely difficult to pack them back. So somehow I managed to roll the smaller bear into the canoe and made way back to town with my wild story. I then also faced the dilemma of the legality of shooting more than one bear however in those days things were a little less complicated in terms of official oversight, although I believe there was one Fish and Game man in town. I somehow talked my dear wife into going and buying a hunting license and that seemed to be the only prospect of legalizing the other bear that was still down on the creek flats. To my surprise and probably after a good deal of coaching and persuasion she accompanied me down the bay in my little 16-foot canoe and we arrived close to where the other bear had fallen. To this day I cannot remember how the two of us were able to roll that bear into that canoe and I would guess his weight was somewhere close to 300 pounds. As anyone who knows when dealing with a canoe they are very tippy and I to this day cannot figure out how we managed that feat. In any event we accomplished that miracle and found ourselves sliding into the small boat harbor in Valdez quite late that night in the darkness. I do remember finding an acquaintance to help extract the bear from the canoe into a vehicle and so there we were stuck with two bears and my first memorable Alaskan experience. Both of them became one of my early taxidermy projects and at some point I gave both of them away to someone. I still have some pictures somewhere that may be appropriate to provide.

Herb Weichert's Bear
Taxidermy by Your's Truly

Lake Telequana

One of my first major expeditions occurred in 1974 and it turned out to be one of the most elaborate and frightening adventures at the time. Again much of it has to be prefaced by our gross inexperience and we indeed learned a lot from that trip. I was accompanied by a fellow employee who I still have kept touch with after all these years. Walter McGehee and his wife, Gail, who were long time employees of the Harborview facility and are currently living in the Springfield, Missouri. This was the first fly-in that I had ever done and with my modest income this was probably a major expenditure. As it turned out this was a rather convoluted expedition via Walter whose first cousin was a major in the air force and had a number of contacts that setup the arrangements. One of which was a gentleman named Louie Brunner who at the time was the preeminent taxidermist in Alaska. Louie was a grand gentleman full of b.s. but was most generous in setting up a number of trips for us and giving me some direction on taxidermy projects. Louie lived on for many years and sold his taxidermy business and specialized in fur buying and was quite a legend at the time in terms of his expertise and knowledge. In any event, Louie was instrumental in giving us direction on how to hunt caribou in the Lake Telequana area, which is located across the Alaska Range approximately 250 miles west of Anchorage. Our first endeavor was to charter an aircraft and we were recommended one called "Big Reds Flying Service" out of Hood Lake in Anchorage. Our pilot fit the imagery of the Alaskan bush pilot, a very weathered character with a large handlebar moustache and I think at that time he was the owner of the air service. Accessing Lake Telequana itself take some doing as you have to go through a number of passes through the Alaska Range, all of which are daunting given whatever weather you might encounter. The particular pass that we chose was Merrill Pass – a winding path through a range of spiraling mountains that at the time was truly astonishing to us. Any wrong turn could end in disaster and there had been more than a few major happenings in the Merrill Pass area. I'm sure that Big Red took advantage of our astonishment and naivety but we were so awe inspired with the venture that we were easy targets for his sarcasm. We asked a number of innocent questions about the dangers of flying through the area and he only looked over with some measure of disdain. One of the obvious and simplified questions was "What would you do if you happened to take the wrong turn through one of these narrow bands of passes?" Without cracking a smile he went on to give us instructions in a very serious manner if indeed we took the wrong turn. As I remember he told us very deliberately to "put your left hand on your left knee and your right hand on your right knee and then bend over and place your head between your legs and when all else fails you can then kiss your ass goodbye". This was followed by a wicked laugh and I'm sure he had told this same line to God knows how many of his patrons throughout the years. When we arrived at Lake Telequana we found Walter's "cousin" and several other gentlemen who were neatly tucked into a comfortable cabin abode. They had decided to take the easy route and weren't going to be tenting it as we were planning. Somehow out of the discussions there happened to be a pilot that they knew that was bringing in supplies for them. Out of that discussion this gentlemen offered to take us out and drop us off in one of the hills where he had been seeing tremendous caribou herds. So without much forethought we loaded the aircraft and then I remember he said, "we'll leave most of your food as I will be back the next day to pick you guys up". Flying off Lake Telequana is certainly a neat experience as it is a very large lake and is now in the Lake Clark National Park, one of the most beautiful parks of Alaska. It is surrounded by the Alaska Range and we found ourselves going the opposite direction to the more low lands and hills in the area. I would guess we flew approximately 40 or 50 miles looking for a site to drop us off.

We ended up finding a small tundra lake that was probably at the 4,000 – 5,000 foot level and it was surrounded as I remember with caribou of all sizes, milling and moving through the area. The pilot arbitrarily picked this small lake and we found ourselves on the shoreline with our gear and one would suspect it was not of the best condition and was mostly army surplus down sleeping bags and I know the tent itself was less than stellar. One learned throughout the years that you do not get dropped into the Alaska bush unless you have premiere equipment particularly your tent that has to be made to weather the most extreme conditions. At that time I remember having my recurve bow in hopes of making a stealthy attack on a caribou and after walking down the edge of the lake I found myself looking at a large milling bunch of caribou and in my excitement to string my bow I misstepped and the limb broke. So there I was on my first Alaskan trip with a broken bow and I was devastated. I did however have my rifle in the tent and that's what we ended up using as this debacle unraveled.

The trip evolved very quickly and the next morning a large herd of caribou came milling through the far end of the lake, more than we ever could have expected. We of course thought that some of the bull caribou were very large and as it turned out they were very mediocre. With abandon and excitement we began shooting at this herd with no regard to what we were doing. To our amazement animals started to drop and we sat in awe as more critters began to hit the ground. They did not immediately respond to the shot as they were running and they were then having a delayed reaction to the impact of the bullet. We kept praying please don't have any more caribou drop over and we were more than a little embarrassed with ourselves. As it turned, out eight animals were on the ground and fortunately the area did have a five caribou limit per person but the magnitude of moving that amount of critter was soon to be tested. The only thing that we had going for ourselves was our youth and strength and Walter was quite a workhorse at the time. I have a very vivid picture of him bent over carrying half a caribou out through the tundra. Those who have walked through tundra know how difficult it can be as it is often wet with hummocks that constantly trip and tangle your legs. I know we spent at least the next two days skinning, gutting and quartering these animals and carrying them back to the far end of the lake. We had no wonder of how we were going to get all of these surplus carcasses back but the pile grew and we just shook our heads on how stupid we had been. This story continued to grind on and became one that I have repeated many times to people, as it was truly a comedy of errors and beginner's ignorance.

1974 - Walter McGehee Struggling

It seems that at least two days after our first onslaught of caribou, six magnificent bulls appeared at the end of the lake and it was clear that these were completely different than the smaller animals that we had taken the first several days. For whatever the reason, I guess the fact that they were truly trophy critters I made my way to the end of the lake and ended up knocking down two of the bigger ones, one of which I still have retained for the memory. These, as noted, were so much larger in body and horn mass that it truly gave us some appreciation of what magnificent animals they were. I believe we skinned both of them keeping the capes for mounting purposes but the bottom line was that it contributed to the massive pile of meat we had already acquired and we were befuddled as to how we would ever salvage all of this given our circumstances, which were getting more dire as the days went by. To say that we were becoming anxious was an understatement and this increased as the days went by. The wind kept pounding on the tent and we lay there for hours wondering what our future would become and whether we would ever see the pilot again. At that time I had the comfort of some good old whiskey and this seemed to salve my anxieties but unfortunately, Walter did not have that option and was reaching panic modes at time despite my efforts to comfort him. Walter, a teetotaler and straight-laced in so many ways had to grin and bear it and he was not doing very well at times. On the fifth day as I remember, Walter was up early and was feverishly cutting alders and had already made a good effort at making an S.O.S. sign on the side of the hill that we were camped on. He actually did a very impressive job and the project was in a manic state to say the least but as it turned out it was an effective effort.

The winds continued to increase it seemed on our little pond and we were speculating at some point as the temperature dropped that it could easily freeze and then that would create a whole new situation in terms of being extricated from our predicament. We climbed up one of the nearby bluffs that gave us a picture of the nearby expanse far below us and for a moment we discussed the prospects of somehow walking out but having no clue of which direction really to go it would have been an absolutely bad, horrendous decision.

It seems that probably a day or so after the big caribou had made their appearance that one evening as we perused the hillside, low and behold a large silver backed brown bear emerged on the far end of the pond and slowly began trudging his way along the bank in our direction. We had little, if any experience with bears, particularly a grizzly bear and as it got closer we thought the worst was upon us. Fortunately at the time he became very close, he

Walter and bear

angled up on the side of the hill and we instinctively decided that we should defend ourselves knowing that we were very vulnerable given the meat that was in the area and our predicament. A volley of shells went out and the bear disappeared into the thick alders.

That night was another long one as we were naively fearful whether the bear was wounded and of course we thought the worst of it might occur if that was the case. So we sat; I'm sure with little sleep until the following morning until we climbed up the hill and fortunately found the animal deceased. We spend a good part of the day skinning the animal and bringing it back to our camp. This bear was subsequently made into a rug and is in Walter's home to this day although, there is a chance he might have donated it to the local school. The bottom line to this whole scenario was that we had more experiences in these three to four days than most people probably have in a lifetime.

Somewhere around the sixth day I believe a small aircraft came by late one evening and he tipped his wings at us to indicate that he had seen our S.O.S. sign and we were given some renewed hope that we might get ourselves out of this predicament yet. The following morning, I believe it was a Sunday, a large C130 aircraft magically appeared over our tent and circled the camp at an extremely low altitude. This is a very large aircraft that the Air Force uses and it's dispatched out of Elmendorf Air Force Base in Anchorage. For a moment I was embarrassed that we had fostered such attention and as the plane continued to circle the tent and the pond out popped several parachutes that fluttered their way down to the alders. We ran like hell to grab the contents and somehow we were able to figure how to operate the radios that were in those packages and were able to communicate with the aircraft personnel as they continued to circle. We explained that we had been dropped off via "Big Red's Air Service" but did not have a clue as to who the pilot was that dropped us to this point. They assured us that they would communicate our distress to someone that might rescue us and were kind enough to ask us if we wanted any additional supplies. As I previously noted, we had left a good portion of our food stash at the main camp in Lake Telequana and although we had God knows how many pounds of caribou we were running out of other rations. Out of the airplane came a large quantity of c-rations so with this we were feeling reassured that our ordeal was to end safely. Unbeknownst to us, the communication that was garbled and was never correctly communicated to the "Big Red's Air Service". He assured them that he had taken care of the problem and he was thinking of some other hunters that he had dropped in the same area and dismissed their distress calls. This indeed would have been a major problem obviously but at the time we were unaware that there was this miscommunication.

The following day, which was I believe was day seven or eight, out of nowhere comes a small aircraft which turned out to be our pilot of over a week ago. He landed with his floats and began to explain that his situation had deteriorated on the big lake and somehow he had punched a hole in one of his pontoons and presumably had made the repair but did not want to take a chance on checking on us with the wind conditions, which were much more severe than what we were experiencing. No doubt we were probably giving him our crazy story and our anxiety of our predicament nonetheless pointing out that we had this large cache of meat that needed to be recovered. At that point, things deteriorated even further than what we had hoped. We loaded the airplane with God knows how much stuff including Walter and several caribou quarters and some of our gear. In his first attempt to get off of this small pond it became crystal clear that he was not going to make it and at the last minute he cut off the engine and almost in this surreal moment the airplane failed to stop in time and ended up rolling up onto the tundra. So there we were with an airplane loaded and sitting in the bushes. Fortunately there was no major damage to the aircraft and I believe in a mad scramble we cut some alders which were certainly not very large and put them under the pontoons as small rollers and somehow between the three of us we were able to wiggle that airplane little by little back into the water. Our pilot, needless to say, was beyond frustrated and said very emphatically that he was not going to take anything but our basic gear and us out of this situation. With some encouragement, we asked him whether we could salvage at least a couple of the two large caribou and the bear hide.

However, the gigantic pile of meat at the end of the lake still remained and I can only take solace in that it probably fed a lot of critters throughout the winter. This represents the only time I have wasted this amount of wildlife and I always have taken pride in recovering everything that we have taken. We did indeed feel very sorry about this as I remember. Arriving back at Lake Telequana, we got a mixed review as to what we had undertaken but indeed were comforted that we had arrived and were going to make it out. There were more delays because of weather and I forget what kind of communication was used to call the air service in Anchorage. This story remains one of the most memorable ones of my career and I'm sure I've told the story multiple times to anyone that might be interested in hearing our debacle. Both of the caribou were mounted and one remains in my home and the other was given to our good friends in Georgetown, Colorado. So ends one of our first major ventures into the Alaskan bush, indeed a story to remember.

Cousin Mike and the $50 Duck Boat

My cousin Mike died last night, October 23, 2017. Mike and his five siblings were as close to family as I had in my growing up years. Mike and I being the same age and in our early childhood spent a good deal of time together. Even during World War II, although I do not remember, my mother and I had lived with them on the east coast while my dad was overseas. Mike and his brother Tom were very close buddies of mine and probably represent as close to siblings as I could have had. As time and circumstances evolved we saw each other much less particularly when they both moved to Seattle and started their various careers. Tom did his duty over in Vietnam and came back a different person in some ways and while he never let on, I'm sure he experienced more than a few serious circumstances and had some post-traumatic symptoms as a result. Mike on the other hand was able to secure a job in graphic engineering for the Boeing Company, however, a serious motorcycle accident in his early adulthood shaped the course of his life. His management of his disability however, made him uniquely extraordinary. He was in the hospital for over a year and it took literally months and months for him to regain his function and he did suffer the loss of one arm, again something that he learned to manage with incredible resignation and patience. He was

Last Photo of Mike in Alaska

always ingenious in the ways to figure out how to deal with self-help skills, much more than I would have, for sure. He worked for years with the Boeing Company and several other aeronautic industries. His devotion to his daughter Heidi was apparent in all he did and certainly this was reciprocated in his later years and Heidi, a physical therapist, made all manners of provisions for her father. Again, I can only remark that Mike's patience and positive attitudes were something I dearly admired in him. He seldom if ever complained and accepted his state with grace and his devotion to the Catholic Church and his faith was always part of his day-to-day routine. His faith grew from his Irish mother who was a staunch Catholic in every way and his mechanical skills came from his dad.

As I thought about Mike in this last day, I harken back to an occasion that would have changed our lives remarkably or may have ended in disaster at a very young age. Mike and I used to do a number of outdoor things and my dad used to take us on various little outings, mostly squirrel and rabbit hunting adventures. However, the story that remains vivid in my memory is one that occurred on a small marshy lake north of Minneapolis probably when we were 17 or 18 years of age. Sometime during that period I had made a purchase of a small homemade plywood duck boat and paid all of $50 for it. It was designed for very small water, mostly for potholes and it had no flotation of any sort and the gunnels were not much more than 10 or 12 inches high and it was not suitable for any type of larger water conditions. It was indeed the most rudimentary floating device that one could imagine but I was tickled to have some means to get out duck hunting.

In any event, we went on a duck hunting venture one afternoon on this very small lake, which I'm sure by now, is surrounded by suburban homes. What I remember most about this was that the lake was shrouded by a marshy bog-like terrain that made it very difficult to access a launching site. As I remember there was only one place that one could drag the boat into open water. As the day wore on I can remember some of the details as we were in the middle of this swampy lake and were trying to find our way back to the launch point. As we crossed the open water which I would guess would be somewhere around a quarter mile wide, to our amazement and horror the boat started filling up with water that was splashing over the gunnels. At some point it was so full of water that it could have gone over at any moment, as we had not been pay-ing attention to what was occurring with the wave action. The good news was that somehow we had the presence of mind to get as low in the bottom of the boat we could be, probably on our knees and we had the brilliant idea to take off our hats and slowly but surely try to bail the boat out a capful at a time. Needless to say if that boat would have gone over we would have been in major problems given the fact that I'm sure we had no flotation devices and we were probably clothed in heavy gear, certainly not suitable for swimming. While both Mike and I probably could have swam some, it would have been a really difficult, if not impossible task to make it to shore.

In any event, as we cautiously bailed the boat we somehow managed to move little by little closer to the shoreline and as the afternoon gave way to almost complete darkness we found our way pulling ourselves along the marshy edge of the lake looking for the opening that would allow us to access the launch area. We had no flashlights and somehow in our youthful naivety we inched our way to safety.

This little story stuck in my mind and I know we had relived this story many times over the years. I know my dear old dad probably shook his head in great dismay when he heard of our stupid mistakes that could have ended both our early lives. For whatever purpose, I hope this little story will be shared at some time with his daughter Heidi whom we still maintain some contact with although she lives in California and I have not seen her for a number of years. Mike's sisters and brother continue to live in Minneapolis and I have mentioned this story to them more than a few times.

One other interesting little tidbit that flashes back in my dim memory is our trip to the veterinarian with the pet duck that we had been taking care of in my back yard in St. Louis Park. At some point in my teen years we decided to raise domestic mallards and even went to the point of building them a small shed to house them during the cold winter months. The dominant little female duck that was one I protected from the more other aggressive birds soon became impaired with some kind of infection, I assumed on her leg. Mike and I in our wisdom at the time decided that this duck needed medical attention and wrapped it in a blanket and walked a mile or two down the highway to the local veterinarian. At that time we had to cross the highway with this crazy little duck and when we arrived at the veterinarians office I remember that the blanket was full of duck poop and was probably quite a sight for those sitting in the waiting area. The veterinarian I can imagine was titillated by the whole situation and decided that a penicillin shot would be in order. I do remember vividly that when my father received a bill from the veterinarian and he was not terribly amused by our decision to seek medical attention for our little bird.

Mike recalled this little story often when we would got together and for whatever reason I thought it would be curious to put some words to it so someone else my share in the amusement of our youthful endeavors.

First Cousins
Mike and Tom Endert

Head-banging on the Dadina Wrangell Mountains Sheep

Sheep hunting is something I made many efforts at doing and had the good company of a number of friends both seasoned and otherwise. In my years there in Alaska I think I took possibly three people who had never sheep hunted before and it turned out they ended up being more successful that I was but that was okay. In the mid 1980's I somehow talked my good friend, Steve Goudreau into taking his first sheep trip that I setup with Lynn Ellis of the Ellis Air Taxi. The Ellis family were longtime Alaskan outfitters and guides. The father being a legend in his time and had several sons who pursued guiding and flying in the Wrangell Mountains, I believe they still have a lodge at the end of the Nabesna Road. The younger brother I believe still does some outfitting but Lynn strictly continues to do his air service and I doubt whether he still flies sheep hunters in at this time. He is a colorful character and I have flown with him several times over the years and always had a glib remark to make about sheep hunting and he has a lifetime of experiences dropping various sheep hunters in various parts of the Wrangell Mountains.

Some of the classic remarks that he always managed to make as we're flying into the hunt area is "Well, boys, if it was easy, women would be doing it" or when we would ask some naïve question about where we were going or how far we had to walk he would always say "Boys, I would suggest that you pack a lunch". The other remark that I seem to remember is his take on sheep hunting and it was always said with a cynical laugh, "Well I quit sheep hunting some time ago because the meat tastes too much like sweat". In any event, I always felt very safe with Lynn and knowing the extent of his experience and knowledge of the Wrangells in particular and I know he's done extensive flying throughout Alaska.

In any event we somehow arrived at the Dadina River drainage on the northwest side of the Wrangell Mountains, just south of the Dadina drainage designated as Sheep Gulch that I believe somehow joins the Dadina drainage. After some reconnaissance we were able to find five rams at the very far end of valley most of which was glaciated rock and didn't look particularly inviting. We concluded that this was going to be indeed a long trek but we undertook the venture with a degree of excitement knowing that at least there would be sheep at the end of the rainbow.

As I recall, I think it took a good two days to walk back into the bowl following an old horse trail probably by one of the old time guides. As we got to the far reaches of the drainage it was time to cross a very fast moving glaciated stream and this is where the problems began. In those days I wore plastic mountaineering boots with inner liners as they give you great side hill traction and they have other advantages in terms of keeping your feet dry. Most of them are made in Austria and Germany and are quite spendy. One of the good advantages of these boots was that the liner could be taken out when you had to cross a stream and you could slide some rubberized slippers inside the boot and make your way across the creeks and streams and then replace them with the inner liner and you have dry feet which is critical when you are covering miles and miles of ground. We could see that this was going to be a bit of a challenge as the water was moving very fast and crossing these streams are very treacherous as you were carrying your pack and rifle and you can expect slippery rocks and the current is pulling at you at varying degrees of intensity. Somehow in our hast I looked over and noted that one of my inner boots was in fact sitting on the top of Steve's backpack. God knows why this happened and as Steve proceeded to make the crossing I could see that that boot was not going to stay on the pack and my yelling was of no avail as the roar of the water precluded Steve from hearing me. Sure enough to my horror I saw the boot fall into the water and it I saw it bobbing down the stream with no chance of ever recovering it. This presented a major problem as the boot shells themselves are essential and walking without them would be almost impossible. Here we were at least eight miles back and still had the trip ahead of us. However, with some improvising, we managed to fashion a boot from extra stockings and some foam rubber that I carried for covering blister areas and some good old duct tape that all created a liner that seemed to work to some degree. This brutalization of my feet probably took its toll and I'm probably paying the price these days with collapsed arches and issues with my toes.

That night we found ourselves hunkered in my small two-man tent pondering what the morning would bring. The next morning we made our somewhat arduous and extremely difficult climb up the vertical rocks to where we had spotted the sheep feeding. Some of the details that follow have been left out for some ethical reasons as our sharp shooting was less than memorable following some miscommunication as to which sheep was to be taken and it was a bit of a scramble to rectify the situation. None-theless we had two sheep down and now the prospects of how we were going to make the return with that many miles ahead of us was difficult to ponder. For anyone who has tried to pack a sheep complete with your gear and rifle, the weight is easily well over 135-150 pounds. The average boned sheep is about 45 pounds depending on the area taken plus the cape and horns push it out to 70 pounds and again with your gear and guns you are carry-ing well over 135-150 pounds. However, in our youth and enthusiasm of the moment we began to struggle slowly back on the trail. I do not remember how we managed to cross that stream with that amount of weight on our backs but somehow we did it but it does not stick in my mind how we accomplished that miracle.

The somewhat hilarious anecdote involving watching Steve climbing through the rocks with his sheep horns on top of his huge pack and in this case, they were not securely fastened. We moved ever so slowly and if we had an occasion to find a seat that we could manage to not completely sit down on we would take advantage of any rest area. However every time Steve would stop or bend over to gasp for air, the horns would roll forward and hit him in the back of the head to the point where he,

Dadina Sheep

at least on a couple of occasions went down to his knees and would shake his head from the stunning blow. I am guessing that we were so exhausted that it didn't seem to make any difference but remains extremely laughable when I think back of this arduous event. I do not remember how many times the head banging occurred but it was more than a few times but as noted, we were so tired that we just didn't have the wherewithal to take off the packs and secure the load correctly. However I note that at some point we did in fact smarten up and properly secure the horns so that poor Stevie didn't have to suffer any further indignations. I believe it took at least two and a half days to return to our beginning point and the landing zone. In that final trek we came upon a very nice grizzly bear that was chewing on the remains of a very large bull caribou, all of which would have been great trophies however we didn't dare think about salvaging either because we knew we did not have the strength to pack them out.

We safely arrived at the landing zone, basically a flat creek bottom area sufficient for landing a Super Cub on tundra tires. Not far from the landing zone was a very nice bull moose rack that somebody had discarded probably for having an overloaded airplane but it was such a beauty that I was able to salvage it and with the help of Lynn he tied it onto the struts of the airplane and I had those hanging at the house for some time. So this will go down as "Head Banging on the Dadina" and I thought it would be worth recalling. Steve never did do the sheep hunting again however we had many many more trips after that mostly to do with waterfowl hunting on our favorite little lake in Valdez. He also was the willing and able to accompany me on many trapping ventures and was always helpful in this regard. He remains to this day one of my fondest friends.

Krista's Black Bear Hunt in Valdez

Krista is our oldest granddaughter and in her growing up years spent many a day with us including most of her summers and Christmas breaks. She showed some interest in trekking behind her old grandfather and we had many day trips checking traps and multiple pictures were taken of her holding the various critters that were taken. However she never actively showed any interest in using a firearm and that was never encouraged. I was always happy with her company and she happily followed me carrying her walking stick and chatting with my dog that was always with me. In her sixteenth year she remarked that she would like to learn how to shoot a rifle and or shoot a bear, which I found more than a bit surprising. We found ourselves out at the local shooting range and to my somewhat amazement she did extremely well even at her early efforts both with the .22 and the larger .30-06 rifle. She seemed to be comfortable with the recoil and hit the target accurately enough that maybe she could in fact accomplish a safe bear venture.

I had been bear baiting off and on for many years in the Valdez area. It was a novelty when I first started doing it and somehow shortly thereafter it became a common occurrence among many of the local people particularly the Coast Guard clan that seems to work in unison. At any event however, it became so popular that all the rules and regulations followed and made life more complicated than I wished to deal with. Some of my favorite little haunts were now off limits and there were rules regarding declaring the spot you were baiting, etc. etc. etc.. One of my favorite places was not that far off the Alyeska Pipeline right of way and I found a natural corridor where the bears would make their way along a hillside and move towards the flats where they would fish when the salmon arrived. I had one particularly neat spot where you could actually sit up on a knoll and be maybe 50 yards above the bottom of the hill in an open area. It took a bit of doing to climb up to this spot but once you got up there it was a very safe location and gave you great visibility.

I believe it was a Memorial Day Sunday when we decided that maybe this was the time to give it a go. I had done some baiting previously but had not done any reconnaissance at to what type of activity was occurring. I had however had some great success in this little spot before so I thought it would be the best way to have Krista try her luck. We dragged ourselves up the very steep little hill complete with my faithful springer spaniel and sat quietly with the bug nets, as it was that time of year when the mosquitos would drive you crazy. It didn't seem like we were there very long when Krista started showing some excitement and saying she saw a bear coming and I often use my little springer to give me some forewarning, as she would pick up the sign and smell before I did. Sure enough as we looked down the way we could see a sizeable black critter making his way towards us. In awe, we watched as the bear got closer and closer and then for whatever the reason he laid down on his stomach and was essentially facing us with his head forward and he was in complete perpendicular alignment. Given this position this was not what one wants to take a shot as the vital areas were covered for the most part and I was in a quandary as to whether I should take a chance with Krista's shooting ability. However, I finally decided maybe if she felt comfortable we could take a shot and remember whispering in her ear saying whatever you do, take your time and be sure that you are exactly on what I tell you. I told her to shoot him right between the ears in the back of the skull area, again this was done with great trepidation as I was most fearful of wounding a bear and in those thick alders recovery is very difficult. After some uneasy moments the gun reported and to my stunned amazement the bear did even make a motion or take a breath. It was like all went silent and for a moment I thought she had missed the bear completely. As we looked down, I could see that the bear was absolutely motionless, not one movement of any part head, nose, nothing, and I was absolutely flabbergasted. I have a picture with her with stunned amazement, as I'm sure she was dumbfounded with what she had done. After some time we concluded that the bear was in fact deceased and found our way down this steep precipice where he lie.

As it turned out upon our investigation the bullet had taken out the brainstem right at the very first cervical vertebrae and that anatomically causes immediate death and shuts down all vital organs, which explains why the bear never even took a breath. In all my hunting escapades I've never seen a shot made with this degree of devastation. This kind of injury would cause immediate death and of course those that suffer quadriplegic accidents suffer similar loss of function when it involves the first two levels of the vertebrae. As it turned out the bear was a very large

Krista's Big One 6'9" - 2000

one probably larger than most bears that I've ever taken and squared somewhere around 6"8". After our bedazzlement we started the arduous process of trying to begin the skinning of the critter and we were in an ugly place with a lot of rotten snow and wet tundra like ground. Fortunately we did have our cell phones along which were somewhat of a new gadget and we were able to call the Goudreau family and not very much later they found their way to us and with a great amount of help we were able to take hide and all of the meat out to where we could transport it. This was Krista's first and only hunting venture with a rifle of any sort and I would doubt that she would ever renew her interest. The bear was subsequently mounted by old grandpa Pat and it is indeed a fine specimen with wonderful hair and great size. Krista's currently living in London with her husband and we have been trying to figure out was that would could transport that animal but the logistics are very expensive and there would probably some customs issues in transporting any wildlife item. Hopefully some day it will find its way to her home.

This remains one of the more memorable experiences that I had with my children and as previously noted the boys never had that much interest, if any, although there were some exceptions.

Archery Hunting for Moose in the Yukon Territory

Somehow I got it in my mind that I wanted to try and go on a bow hunting trip to the Yukon Territory. The Yukon still today remains one of the truly last frontiers and has I think I total population of less than 50,000 residents and the amount of commercial guiding is just a minor fraction compared to the over-harvesting that has occurred in Alaska. The Yukon today probably has some of the finest trophy animals available however the expense of securing a guide has become astronomical. At one point the Yukon Territory had less than twenty guides compared to the seven hundred plus guides that are pillaging the existing Alaska resources. The unfortunate comments on the Alaska guide situation is that many of them do not live in the state and they exploit the trophies, probably do not pay taxes and then return to their home states.

Somehow I got the name of an outfitter that worked out of the small village of Carmacks, Yukon Territory approximately 100 miles northwest of Whitehorse on the Yukon River. The gentleman's name was Don Marino, not to be confused with the famous quarterback of football fame Dan Marino. This fellow turned out to be one of the finest gentlemen that I could have asked for. I've had less than sterling experiences with some of the guides in the northern hemisphere, as most of them tend to be pretty helter-skelter and not very professional. In any event I made a deal with Don if we helped take down his camp that he would allow us to come in for a late season moose hunt at his base camp on Bonnet Plume Lake, a long narrow lake that sits very close to the McKenzie Mountains that borders the Northwest Territories.

I was accompanied by my good friend George Maykowskyj and I think with some reluctancy he agreed that this would be worth undertaking giving the reduced price of the hunt and the fact that neither of us had hunted in the Yukon Territory. I would be remiss if I did not talk a little about George and his wife, Judy. The remain one of our finest friends and we still maintain contact with them even though they currently live in Spokane. We met

Bonnet Plume Lake

them in early on in the 1970's – George being a teacher
and Judy working for the Department of Transportation.
George soon made his way up the hierarchy of the school
district and eventually became the superintendent. In my
humble estimation I always viewed George as being one
of the most multi-talented persons that I had have had
the good fortune of befriending. He is a ball of energy and

ambition even to this day. Always building and improving his circumstances and his true love is in making repairs and renovations of his home in Spokane. I believe he was in the Valdez school district for twenty years then moved on to head up the school district in McGrath, a very rural area northwest of Anchorage and covered a multitude of small villages in the various river systems. George always seems to do everything well from his athleticism to running a charter boat service in the Valdez Sound, which he did for many years. He was always constantly building, fixing and restoring almost anything that came upon him from vehicles to boats to home structures. Over and above that, George and Judy involved themselves in all manner of civic and social activity in the Valdez community and they were indeed a positive force wherever they went.

George and I took off down the road to Whitehorse approximately 800 miles from Valdez in a borrowed Jeep for some reason and soon found ourselves flying down the Yukon River in a large amphibious airplane–I believe it was a Turbo Otter. It was a long trip and we were indeed fully loaded with gear. As noted, the Bonnet Plume Lake is a long narrow body of water that seems to be at least 10-15 miles long and it was very close to the MacKenzie Mountains that are famous for their remote and beautiful scenery. The one beauty of the Yukon Territory is that you seldom see any other aircrafts or people and it is truly a remote and isolated part of the world. Unfortunately, this cannot be said of Alaska where you can hardly go anywhere without seeing other aircraft.

Arriving at Bonnet Plume Lake we were greeted by Don and his right-hand man, a fellow named Roger, and as it turned out his crew of wranglers were in the process of taking all of the horses out for the winter. This was indeed a mind boggling undertaking as they had to take I'm guessing 20 horses approximately 200 miles to the nearest road site and this involved crossing several major tributaries on route. This was going to be indeed a daunting task and most of these cowboys had been in this area for almost three months so I'm sure they were anxious to get back to civilization and were also concerned about the onset of early winter conditions that would make their exodus more complicated for sure particularly if the rivers started to freeze. As I recall, George's little cache of whiskey went up in flames probably within the first hour that he arrived as he generously offered it to the local cowboys there who hadn't seen liquor for some time.

For the most part, Don and his assistant guide Roger let us do our own thing, which was kind of the way we preferred it. We didn't need to be nurse-maided as we both had a fair amount of experience in the bush. They did however, give us a tour of some of the areas and we did have the use of a canoe that allowed us to transfer from one end of the lake to the other although most of our time was spent near the north end of the lake which narrowed to a point and exited with a river drainage and a natural squeeze point for any movement of moose through the area. This was during the rutting season in mid to late October and the bulls would be moving about at that time looking for cows. So for the first few mornings we found ourselves positioned on the hillside near the very end of the lake, which again was the natural narrowing point. As I recall we had hardly been there more than a few hours when a bull moose showed itself and was walking parallel to our position and both George and I proceeded to get in front of the animal as it made it's way through the alders. For whatever reason, out of excitement I really didn't give a good look at the size of the moose but it presented itself in such a wonderful broadside manner than an arrow flew and to my amazement it fell over as if shot by a rifle. It was an outrageous site and I was shaken by what an arrow could do. As it turned out, the arrow had hit the moose directly in the spinal column between two vertebrae and it was pure accident that it did not walk away unscathed as an arrow and inch above that would have gone into the loin and would not have been a fatal shot at all and a shot below would have also been in a non-lethal area. That arrowhead is still embedded directly in the middle of that spinal column today and I often show it to people of interest. The downside of the story is that it was only a very small bull but it was a bull moose so we were grateful to have the meat and the experience.

The real crux of this story lies with the following adventures that ensued. The next day I found myself sitting above the carcass in hopes that a wolf might make his appearance but that was not the case. George on the other hand, checked out the remains within the next day or so and low and behold there was a wolverine feeding on the carcass. According to George and with some detail, he did an extraordinary slow stalk and let an arrow fly hitting the animal not once but twice which was a remarkable feat of shooting. Believe me there are seldom if any recorded incidences where a wolverine was taken by archery equipment as they are very elusive and seldom seen, let alone being able to get that close for an archery shot. Most wolverines weight approximately 30-40 pounds and are of very short stature and do not present much of a target for sure. This indeed was a marvel to the guides who had never seen such a thing and George was elated with his accomplishment.

The next day I found myself sitting above the kill area in hopes that another predator might make an appearance. Also on that particular day George came walking by and going further up the river with Roger in hopes of finding a moose. As I was quietly sitting by the carcass here comes the trophy moose that we were expecting to see and of course it would have been a relatively easy bow shot for sure and I estimated that he was well in the 60-inch range. I quietly said to myself, "God I hope you're watching what's going on George, this moose is coming right your way up the riverbank."

I spent several hours with nothing of consequence and found my way back to the basecamp pondering what had occurred with George. I can vividly remember him coming back down the lakeside head bent over with dismay and discouragement. The story unfolded with some detail and with great frustration. As George told the story they were about to have a little lunch on the riverside when they looked over and sure enough that large bull moose that I had seen earlier made his appearance directly in front of them and George proceeded to let arrows fly and he was apparently discombobulated to the point where his aim was not true. He said the one arrow went over the back of the animal, one went in a non-vital area and one final arrow ended up stuck in the antlers themselves. He could not explain how

Yukon with George Maykowskyj

this all occurred but it was truly a disappointment as he had a grand chance for the trophy that we had come to see. Here he had made the most outrageous shots on a small target and then failed for whatever reason to make it come true on an animal that weighed probably in the 1500-pound range. Thus our trip to Bonnet Plumes soon came to an end and the weather got progressively colder and I believe at one point it was well below zero and the prospects of the lake freezing was for real. We scrambled to assemble a mountain of gear, mostly saddles and tents, etc. and when the plane finally arrived it was a larger amphibious aircraft that we literally packed to the ceiling and somehow we were able to squeeze ourselves in on top of the gear all of which was not particularly safe conditions of overloading airplanes has always been one of the major sources of aircraft disasters. However, in the Alaskan bush one has to make due with taking chances, as often you did not have any choice in the matter.

George was invited to Alaska Bow Hunting Association banquet and was awarded some type of recognition for his feat at taking a wolverine, something I'm sure that had never been done. He even shook the hands of the somewhat infamous character of note, the one and only Ted Nugent who is a very controversial right-wing activist.

That wolverine to this day is still in George's house in Spokane and I think we both put it together and made it look like a presentable trophy complete with some ptarmigan. Our Yukon trip is one I would like to repeat, however time, age and money will probably preclude that from every happening. There are still some great areas to hunt in the Yukon Territory but the financial costs of hunts these days become almost out of my realm of possibility, unless I win the lottery.

The African Queen

One of my earliest moose ventures was in September of 1974 and again it was coordinated through my contacts with the then famous taxidermist and fur dealer, Louie Brunner. I somehow wanted to put together a float trip and I'm not sure what the impetus was to pick this particular drainage but it was in fact out of the village of Pilot Point which is approximately 200 plus miles down the Alaska Peninsula. It is where some of the biggest moose in the state have been taken for many years. The particular little tributary was called Pumice Creek and it flowed into the bay on the opposite side of Pilot Point. We secured the services of one of the local air taxis, a gentleman named Johnny Ball and as I remember he had several brothers in the air taxi business and he knew the area well. With the generosity of Louie who lent us two of his rafts, we took a commercial aircraft down to Pilot Point. Walter McGehee again agreed to come along even after our fiasco of the previous year that was chronicled in my story of the Lake Telequana nightmare. I believe we landed in a wheeled plane miles up from the ocean and I recall flying up the winding river. I do not know how many actual miles were involved in the float but I'm sure we had asked the question and in our naivety we did not know what type of undertaking we were getting ourselves into. We landed up in some high ground and started the arduous unloading process and inflating the rafts and dragging all of the equipment down to the river's edge. I can't remember how far that distance was but again our youth and enthusiasm probably overcame the work involved just to do that. I remember the first day or two of our float was relatively easy although the water was faster than what we would have liked and we were whisking by prime moose areas at a rate that made it difficult to scout. I believe probably on the third day or so the river wound down into some lower elevations and the float trip took on a much slower pace. Somewhere within the first few days, once we got into some marshy lowlands, we happened upon a group of cow moose and we were signaled by an aircraft that was circling and had obviously seen something of note.

There was in fact a large group of cow moose. I believe the number was 12-13 and with them was a solitary bull. After a relatively short stalk the first bull moose of the trip was down and then of course the work of dismembering, boning, etc., which was not an unfamiliar task began. Working in the muskeg was never easy and dragging large pack-fulls of meat to the rafts was difficult indeed. I do not remember how far that moose was from the riverside but it probably was farther than we would have liked. The size of the moose was somewhere in the 50-inch range and at the time I was excited that it was a trophy, although in retrospect, it was a relatively small bull.

The magnitude of what we finally ended up discovering on this trip was yet to be played out. Loading those rafts with the meat and our gear was already obviously going to be an issue. We had included in our gear my father's old 1957 5-horse Johnson motor; a relic in its time, but at it turned out it was paramount in this trip. Without it we would have been in dire straits as things materialized. I often recall how my dad took meticulous care of his few sporting items and this little motor was the apple of his eye and it hardly had a scratch on it. There I was probably brutalizing it by dragging it though God knows what kind of conditions and certainly did not have the respect for it that I should have. The dependability and tenacity of that little motor was demonstrated 10-fold as the trip took on more magnitude and ultimately desperation.

A note of interest and as the experience developed, those people in the interior of Alaska that depend on moose would not think of shooting a moose beyond 75-yards from the river and they have learned through the millenniums that the work involved is beyond what

Walter McGehee

they would care to deal with. So it is only the dumb old white man that ends up shooting animals so far away that it creates a major strenuous ordeal.

Following the loading of our rafts, we again started our journey downstream and I believe it was the following day that a more sizeable bull moose was standing on the shoreline and Walter dispatched it with one shot and an interesting consequence was that the moose stood up on his hind legs and went completely backwards impaling it's antlers deep into the mud. I've only seen this happen on one other occasion and it obviously had to do with the bullet placement somewhere in the spinal column. In one way it was easier to disembowel the animal given its position but on the other hand I remember extracting that critter from the deep mud was an issue. Fortunately this moose was considerably closer to the river's edge and it made the loading of the rafts much more easy, however the load now approached the 1,000-pound range and it became blatantly obvious that we were going to have some issues transporting this amount of mass down this relatively small creek that was diminishing in its levels as we went. It became frighteningly obvious that the water level was going to haunt us for the remainder of the trip. Thus began the "African Queen" scenario of towing the rafts by hand, which I believe went on for several days. Fortunately Walter was in great shape although as it turned out he ended up with a hole in his hip boots that kept his feet in icy cold water for several days with no repair in sight. I don't know how many days of actual physical hauling we did but I know it was almost beyond our capacity. I know at one point we seriously considered unloading some of the meat but could not bring ourselves to waste any of this, however it appeared that we may not have a choice. At times the river got extremely narrow and again the depth of the river was only a few inches at times and I know we strained to the point of blood vessels popping from our foreheads as we tried to navigate this amount of weight down the creek. Somewhere within the next day or two the water level magically seemed to rise and I'm assuming it had to do with the tidal action from the ocean and we were hitting some high tide overflow. We hit another tributary and that probably added to the water level that we so desperately needed. It would be well to note that we should have had better topographical maps so that we could have more clearly plotted our course but again, poor preparation and inexperience was obvious. As we got into deeper water I was able to start our little outboard and chugged a long faithfully for it seems forever but then as we hit shallower stretches it would suck up sand into the impeller and it would overheat and shut

Your's Truly

down. We had to wait considerable time for it to cool and
once again it would start and I know we did this it seems
like one hundred times but again, a testament to how well
those old motors were made. As we got down further we
were unable to have a clue as to how close the ocean outlet
was and we were surrounded by high weeds that gave us
no way of viewing what was in front of us. Again this was

reminiscent of the classic movie, The African Queen, where they tried to find their escape to the lake but they had no idea where they were heading or how long it would take to reach open water. What we really didn't fully understand was that the tidal movement was stronger than the current of the natural stream and it was forcing us backwards, thus the importance of our little motor. That little 5-horse kept perking only despite numerous stoppages when it would overheat and considering it was pushing two rafts side-by-side with well over a thousand pounds of weight is astounding when I think about it now. I don't know how many hours it took but at the time it seems like eternity as we pushed downstream against the tidal action. Every time that we restarted the motor after it overheated I was amazed that it was still running. At some point I think we found deeper water that did not create the same overheating issues that we had in the areas where we were hitting sandbars and at some point we finally emerged from the tangled web of willow and low and behold we found ourselves at the open ocean of the Ugashik Bay. One little tidbit as we were coming down the river at some point with meat and horns protruding from the raft another moose emerged and saw this carnage as another moose and it being the rutting season this particular moose walked directly to us and would have been indeed a great opportunity for a bow shot. We actually had to stand up and scare this particular bull moose away, which I wish we could have had on tape but we did not have that type of paraphernalia in those days. As we found the Ugashik Bay outlet we also found a small type of cabin suspended by stilts that we took refuge in. The mud in that area was horrendous and all we could do was pull the two rafts with all that weight up on to the mud flats as best as we could and leave everything as is and fumble our way into this little abode. At that point we were just relieved to have a comfortable place to lay down in and we thought we had at least arrived. After perusing the area it because blatantly apparent that the expanse of ocean was signifi-cant and we were on the opposite side of the Ugashik Bay area with the village of Pilot Point being God knows how many miles away but I'm guessing 3-5 miles and we had no idea of how were going to transverse that amount of water with our condition of two rafts and a tiny motor. Our predicament became even more complicated as the evening brought the darkness of the night and all of sud-den we were hit with an outrageous windstorm that shook us to our very inners. I swear the winds had to have been over 80-miles per hour and this tiny little abode being held up by four timbers shook and I remember holding on for dear life as we tried to stay on the floor of this cabin

The Ordeal - Pilot Point, Alaska

wondering if it was going to go over. One twist of fate that worthy of note was that particular evening we had made the decision to try to make our way across the bay to the Pilot Point side and as it turned out, the little Johnson motor finally gave up the ghost approximately 100-yards from the shoreline. Somehow we managed to paddle our way back to the shore. The wind that came up that evening would have indeed created a situation that could have been fatal and we could have been blown to oblivion given the situation we had with no power and the amount of weight in these two small rafts so it was more than a bit ironic that the motor finally quit at the most opportune time and there we were stuck in this little cabin sustaining a wind storm that was epic. A little further trivia to this storm was that the same storm eventually moved into the south central area of Alaska and into our hometown of Valdez and actually blew down the construction of the Totem Inn that very night or the night after. When we left, all of the framing had been completed and the building itself was quite large – one of the first major buildings put up after the move to New Town Valdez. As it turned out the entire structure was flattened and they had to start anew. A little further bit of history was that the Totem Inn, which was the hub of all activity in Valdez, was recently completely renovated and a new hotel was built as of this past year. That night of the storm was still something I remember and Walter was more shaken that I was and swearing that he would never get himself in such a predicament again. The building shook and swayed and we had neither reprieve nor sleep. Unfortunately we did not have the luxury of having a satellite phone at that time which would have been very important. To this day I often rent a satellite phone as it certainly allows for some emergency communication that may be necessary in such outings. During the day or two that we stumbled around our windswept abode I recall sneaking up on a large flock of Canadian geese and God knows with three shots, seven geese come tumbling down and I dragged them down to the cabin and also managed to shoot a red fox that came by so God knows why I was accruing more carnage but again my youth and exuberance doing whatever was out of control I guess. Somewhere in the next several days as we were wandering aimlessly around our small cabin we noted that an airplane was circling approximately a mile away and we went into full gear waving our arms and trying to get their attention. As it turned out the pilot must have landed and we discussed our predicament and that Johnny Ball was the person that dropped us off and pleaded that they let him know that we were in this situation. So once again we were hopeful that we could be rescued and I believe the next day or so a skiff of sorts appeared with a young native fellow who had said that he had spent the entire evening and day finding his way down from the village of Ugashik to where we were situated. Obviously the communication had gotten to Johnny and he had sent this young fellow. Needless to say as in good native fashion he had minimal gear, no life jacket, no jacket to speak of and he said he had spent the night sleeping on the boat, which again was probably a skiff of no larger than 18-foot. So began the project to unload the rafts and pile them into the boat and off we went to Pilot Point. Somewhere not too far out of the bay area I remember that he must have hit an obstruction and sheered a pin and in a very nonchalant fashion he looked around his wooden boat and took out a nail and proceeded to improvise a sheer pin, again a testament to the resourcefulness of the folks that live in that country. Upon our return to Pilot Point we were, needless to say, very relieved and did not fully understand what an expanse of water we would have had to have cross. I think we gave every bit of cash we had in our pockets to this native fellow along with our appreciation for his efforts to bail us out of the situation. For those that are unaccustomed to this country, those that live in it are very nonchalant in dealing with these situations and seldom give much thought to how to improvise and make due. At some point thereafter we loaded all of our gear and moose into a Cessna 207 which is a relatively large single engine airplane with a lot of freight capacity and we found ourselves back to King Salmon. I remember going to the local Alaska Sausage Company which is still in operation today and in those days the expense of processing meat was minimal and I think we returned to Valdez with something like eight hundred wieners and I don't know how many hundreds of pounds of burger and other pieces we had. This is one of the more memorable outings that I have clear memory of and unfortunately Walter was the victim of my planning and I don't think after this trip that Walter and I had many more ventures as I think he arrived at the fact that this was more than he wanted to deal with. The good thing is that we both survived and went on to live our lives for whatever its worth and all we have is distant memories.

Saginaw Bob and the Maple Syrup

This story begins with a rather strange little anecdote involving Mr. Bob Erwin, more famously referred to as Saginaw Bob. He is the father of one of our best friends Sara Goudreau-Erwin. Bob is from the upper Michigan area and the family grew up in that part of the country with at least several of the daughters moving to Alaska. Bob is known to be a very gregarious gentleman with a deep hearty voice and known for telling tall tales and probably embellishing some of his adventures. In any event, he has been a sportsman most of his life and used to take a lot of trips and travels often coming to Alaska to visit his daughters. On one of his last visits to Valdez I happened to meet him in front of the Goudreau home and he was about to load up to return to Michigan. In a generous moment he handed me a classic old jug of maple syrup that came from his home area and wished me good luck as he was about to embark on his long ride home. This was somewhere around the month of May and the bear season was beginning shortly as we always look forward to that time of year. For many a season I used to trek up the hill to an area that was adjacent to the border of the Alyeska Pipeline, which is now highly secured. In those days things were not as serious but after "9/11" things changed dramatically. I had a favorite spot that I used to sit and a number of bears were taken from this spot. It was a canyon-like drainage that went up parallel with Solomon Lake and it was always a neat place to sit and watch the hillside. At times I did bait there, as it was a natural hump that you could put a bait below that and be in good position if any bear would come that way. I also spent many a day climbing the hill to that particular spot for the purposes of trapping, mostly martin.

In any event, I took off on a bright morning which I believe was Memorial Day of 2001 and there was still plenty of snow on the ground as that side of the bay always was late in melting out as the sun would not effect the south side of the bay like it did on the Valdez side. At that point all of the alders were still under snow but with one lowly large black spruce. As I made my way with my snowshoes and my old faithful dog, Q.T., I noticed some very large bear tracks that were half melted out but heading in my same direction and I speculated that they had been made the day before. I should note that I had, the previous week been up the same hill and hung Saginaw Bob's syrup on a tree branch not far from this large spruce tree. As I arrived that day I could see that the jug had been chewed on and didn't quite know what to make of it. I found a comfortable spot right below the spruce tree and settled into glass the hillside. What is interesting is that with the snow conditions, the bows of the spruce are often covered in the lower sections and actually form an umbrella type of canopy. As I sat there and stared up at the hillside I detected some strange wheering noise that I thought was the wind picking up off the ocean. The dog didn't seem particularly alarmed, which was very strange but it was unsettling to the point that I got up and made a trek around the tree to see if I could see anything inside of the bows. As I approached the front of the tree I peered in and to my startled amazement all I saw was a large black nose, probably within 5-feet of where I was sitting. I was more than a bit dumbfounded began to back track and as it were, one of my snowshoes came off and I was scrambling to retreat. This was indeed a predicament as it turned out because that bear could have grabbed me by the back of the neck at any point but possibly the dog's presence kept it at bay.

I remember dropping down and going to a little adjacent hillside and sat momentarily and within minutes out emerged this vary large black bear swinging his head back and forth with some agitation. Instinctively and with one shot the bear came rolling down the hill and I found myself standing over it with some degree of amazement, as it was an extremely large bear. The largest I had ever taken in my career. I took a number of pictures but was scratching my head as to how to get this large bear off of the hillside. I quickly decided I should call the Wade brothers and tell them of my situation. They are world-class snow machine

The Big One 7' - Close Encounter

132

Ricky Wade to the Rescue

gents and their family grew up in Valdez and they have a wealth of experience in the woods and I have several stories of their exploits as this scenario continues. Within a very short time I could hear snow machines roaring in the distance and when they arrived we loaded the bear up which I'm guessing was well over 300-pounds and we made our way down to where we could load it into a vehicle. As it turned out, the bear scored over 19-inch skull and was a true 7-foot length bear from nose to tail and had a gorgeous hide that was perfect in all ways. That bear subsequently mounted life-size and was one of my finer taxidermy efforts and was later put on display.

So the story of Saginaw Bob's syrup came to quirky end and I retrieved the gnarled jug giving it to Sara. I'm sure there was a fair amount of laughter and the story was communicated to Bob. Not too many years after this story, Bob passed away in Michigan and I believe Sara brought that chewed up jug to his memorial service and I can imagine there was lots of chit chat about the circumstances. So ends the tale of the maple syrup and the big black bear of Solomon Gulch.

Blood and Guts
(Boog's Moose)

In the fall of 1981 I had successfully drawn a coveted moose tag that was down on the Kenai Peninsula. These permits are highly sought for as it is a trophy area and there are stipulations in terms of the size of the moose that can be taken. There are approximately six or seven areas with very few tags in each of the areas. I drew a tag with my son, Patrick, on what was called Indian Creek. It was located off of one of the large lakes in the area, Lake Tustumena. It is a large expanse of water and not far from that is a lake called Lake Skilak, also a very large body of water that is the headwaters of the famous Kenai River that flows into the ocean. So it was with some degree of excitement that we drew such a tag but the logistics of how to proceed was always going to be one that would take some planning. After a number of phone calls, one of them with the local Fish and Game office, I was told that you would need a packer that had horses as the moose area was well above the lake and transporting gear and a moose would be arduous undertaking as there are no motorized vehicles allowed. I believe my son Patrick was age 16 at that time and still had interest in hanging around with his old man. We had at least one other trip of note, that being a caribou hunt in the Wrangell Mountains. As I did my homework I found that there were a number of packers in the area and the most notable one was a fellow named Jerry Farewell who called his operation "Blood and Guts Packing". As it turned out he lived on Lake Tustumena and was a Vietnam vet and I suspect had found some peace of mind in the seclusion of his cabin on the lake. That particular trip occurred in the latter part of October which was going to be fraught with weather issues and in this case it was as there was a very early snowfall that covered all of the Anchorage area and all the way down the Kenai Peninsula. The temperatures were also dropping appreciatively. Jerry's mother was an operator of a convenience store and I believe she was the one that directed us down to the lake landing area where Jerry arrived in a small aluminum skiff. I thought, my God, this is a pretty small boat given this large water and I know how the wind can raise havoc and we had to travel approximately 5-10 miles down the lake as the drainage we had access too was the farthest one. Jerry, I would guess was in his 40's and bearded but looked like he knew what he was doing and had the experience for what he did as source of income. I would guess that he also did some trapping and other things including collecting antlers in the spring for sale to the tourists.

Jerry, as it turned out was a great guy and went above and beyond his duties to make sure that Patrick and I were safe. He did so much as to even help us follow a rather poor trail that led up to the treeline where he said the moose spent their time. The treeline is always the key area as it does break into willows and alders, which is the prime food source for the moose. The heavy black spruce closer down to the lake have little for them to eat on. That trek up the hill was not fun and I think it was approximately 6-miles of uphill walking with gear and fortunately Jerry carried the tent that was in itself a bit of a handful. I believe we would have had trouble finding our way up that trail as it was not clearly distinctive by any means and just followed a creek bottom. When we arrived up in the tree line there was some obvious places for setting up our tent, which was an older one that was less than suitable for these conditions but was the only one I owned at the time.

This was during the time when the rut was probably still in full throttle although often the end of October sees the end of the rutting activity. The snow was approximately 6 to 10-inches deep and make trekking about more difficult. Jerry left us with a salute and good wish and said he would be back in a few days or I think even longer. As the days began, the nights got colder and I think we also received another 6-inches of snow that did everything but take the tent down. Our nights became very miserable and everything was wet and clammy. Hanging on a tree not far from us was a an old Coleman lantern. The glass mantle was broken but it still was functional. This lantern as it turned out, made all the difference in making this trip bearable as we had sufficient fuel along and we kept that lantern going at night and it was a source of warmth and security. From that point forward, I never took a fly-in trip without bringing a lantern. It is something I almost insist on when I make any venture and it has come in more than a little handy on a number of other hunting trips. Patrick or Boog as we referred to him was pretty stalwart in hanging in there as the days went by I did remember climbing that hill was a good test of his tenacity and at times he was losing confidence in his strength to carry his heavy pack and trudge forward. I know we spent at least three days wandering the tree line and always keeping in mind where out tent was as we did not to lose sight of that given how cold it was becoming at night, I'm guessing somewhere in the 20 degree range if not colder.

Unbeknownst to us, shortly after this snowfall covered all of our gear and tent, Jerry had made a trip up to check on us which we did not know and he was a bit alarmed that we were not there and he was thinking that something could have gone amiss. For him it meant a trip down lake from his cabin which was considerably far down the lake and trekking the round trip of 12-miles up and down that God-awful hillside. Somewhere around the fifth day I believe we were giving up hope as we had hardly seen little sign of moose activity let alone a moose itself. However, on the one fog-shrouded morning there across the hillside was a sizeable bull moose standing broadside. I remember scrambling with great enthusiasm and sternness and telling Boog to get ready to make a shot as the bull was well within range. I believe we both laid down and moments later the guns went off and the moose went down. It was with great elation that we had achieved that we had come for but now lay the task of dismembering this huge critter and I still remember with amazement that I did it with the help of a very small pocketknife with a 3-inch blade. This truly was a poorly equipped situation as one needed to have excellent cutting instruments as the hide itself is so thick and you're dealing with well over 500-pounds of meat. At that time I had the youth and vigor to work hard and I believe I had that entire animal skinned and boned in about four hours which is quite a feat. Boog's hands were extremely cold and I remember him putting his hands inside of the body cavity for warmth.

Now we were faced with the prospects of what to do with this gigantic pile of meat including the antlers, which were trophy size, somewhere in the 55-inch range but had wonderful confirmation and many points. A number of the tines were broken off and speculated that this moose probably got beat up by the really large one over in the next valley and had retreated to this area after his ordeal. One of the tines was dangling and so I'm guessing he took quite a beating. When we had disemboweled that moose I found the heart which is all of 5 or 6-pounds at least and to my amazement was a large hole, dead center in the heart so we were pleased with our performance.

We returned to our tent and it was probably the following day that Jerry arrived to check on us. This was his third trip up the hill and of course, we told him of our success which involved him returning again all the way to his cabin on the lake and loading up his horses and taking them down the shoreline and we're talking logistically a long ways and then coming up the hill to retrieve the moose

Cold Morning But a Smile of Success - Oct. 1986

and gear. His partner was a very tall, rugged looking gentleman who carried a sawed off shotgun that he had made into a pistol and apparently there were more than a few instances where brown bears would pick up the smell of their load and they had to deal with that situation. The bears on the Kenai Peninsula seems to be more aggressive as they've had many encounters with humans and there have been more than a few maulings and deaths. It seems almost every year there is one major bear incident on the

Kenai. So "Blood and Guts Packing" did their job and we followed behind the pack train but I cannot remember how we faired once we got to the lake as we had to wait until he could return with the boat. We spent a night at his cabin and we were more than a bit grateful for the extraordinary effort that Jerry had put out for us and his concern for our safety. I paid him extra money for his hard work, the amount being so much less that what they now charge for such services. So Jerry and his partner remain in mind's eye as being one of the good guys of our experience in the wilderness and I would speculate that maybe Jerry's military service has much to do with pride and concern about his comrades in arms and served as a basis for his extraordinary help with this trip.

One sad anecdote to this story was approximately a year or two after our trip down the Kenai, Jerry's mother was shot and killed at her convenience store and it was not until 25-years later that they actually apprehended the fellow that committed the crime. I've never talked to Jerry since that time but did write him some thank you letters when we returned to Valdez. So ends the story of the "Blood and Guts Packing" operation and that moose hung in our house in Valdez and was one of our treasured trophies given that ordeal that we went through. It was one of the few exciting adventures that I was able to share with my son, Patrick.

Father-Son Caribou Adventure in the Wrangell Mountains

In the 80's there was a sizeable caribou herd that made their trek around the Wrangell Mountains up near Glennallen and these mountains are some of the highest ones in the state. Mount Wrangell, Mount Drum and two others that I believe are in the 17,000 to 18,000-foot range. This particular herd was one that was easily attainable in terms of the permit process and everyone in town at that time seemed to be able to get one. Subsequently, however what happens in many situations, is that the herd disappeared and probably find their way into the larger Nelchina herd. In any event, it was a reasonably easy hunt to access although again it required the use of an air service as it was a good 40 to 50-miles from the main highway to where the herd used to make their way. On this particular trip we joined forces with my best buddy, George Maykows-kyj and his son, Mike. Mike and my son, Patrick were the best of friends and went through all of their grade school, high school and college careers together. Unfortunately, this all came to a tragic end following Mike's graduation from college when he was involved in a shooting while working part-time in Spokane. This was a trauma that the family and I suspect also my son, has never resolved but I thought it would certainly be worthy of note. We secured the services of one of the local air service fellows of great note, namely Ken Bunch. Ken had a long history of guiding and was now just in the latter years of his career and was mostly doing short air taxi trips. Not many years after this trip, fate took its course Ken died of a heart attack while trying to extricate his airplane from a glacier and overexerted himself to the point where it caused his demise. In any event, he was considered to be one of the most reliable air services in the area and he took us into what they call Dry Lake, a lake bed that had dried up and provided a great landing area as it was flat and without brush. We were cloaked by some very dramatic mountains and it was an idyllic setting. I think the first day or so we managed to shoot a few ptarmigan and we started out our venture having cooked them on an open fire.

The hunt began as we decided to break up and go in

opposite directions. I was with my .22 and Patrick with a borrowed gun that proved to be quite an undoing unbeknownst to us until we were well into the hunt. As I recall it was a relatively small caliber, probably a .308 and I believe it was a Remington model that I later found out had a long history of serious defects. This unfortunately was the case with this particular gun as we were soon to find out. As we wandered down from our campsite we had several encounters with small bunches of caribou and Boog excitedly tried his hand at a few shots, however it was blatantly apparent that there was a serious malfunction with the gun. When the safety was released the gun fired without pulling the trigger and of course it made it extremely dangerous and frustrating. After several aborted attempts and taking shots at various caribou we were betwixt and between about what to do. The frustration grew in my son's face as he suffered some major discomfort in his thumb as the recoil of the gun would come back and I'm sure hurt like hell. I believe we wrapped it up somehow and decided that we would try to carefully avoid getting his fingers in the trigger mechanism and shoot the gun by aiming it using the safety as a trigger. It was a very clumsy way of starting his big game hunting career but we tried to make due with what we had. Several more attempts were made and misses occurred as he became more gun shy of the recoil and the discomfort with each shot. As I remember we were down to one final shell and we continued to make our way down the mountainside not knowing really what to do. At about three of four in the afternoon when the sun was beginning to drop we found a lone bull caribou standing in a dried up tundra pond and we agreed this was going to be our last chance at success. I believe I even tried to engage my little .22 but I know we talked seriously about aiming as best as he could and hoping for the best.

To our surprise and elation the caribou went down and we had achieved success despite all of the tribulation.

We did some skinning of the caribou but knew we were running out of daylight and thought it best to find our way back to the main campsite. I made the dumb mistake of leaving my pack somewhere up on the hillside and as it turned out it was a camouflaged color, which I kicked myself now for getting one as it is easily disguised and hard to find in the tangle of alders. This preoccupation with camouflaged clothing these days is crazy. Every nimrod has to be dressed head to toe with some crazy camouflaged stuff and I'm personally sick of it. In any event, having a camouflaged pack on the side of the mountain was not a great help in finding it. After considerable looking we gave

Mike Maykowkyj & Boog Cleaning Ptarmigan

up on it and carried head and horns back over my head and tried to find our way back up the mountainside. This became increasingly difficult as the sun was going down and we had no clear markers and were at times feeling more than a bit desperate that we were lost. In our hurry to make a stalk on this caribou we had failed to look back as one should and try to get a handle on landmarks that could be used to retrace your steps. Again a very obvious thing that one does when you're out in the bush or for that fact, any outing in unfamiliar country. Somehow we managed to find the camp, probably because the Maykowskyjs had a lantern going and a fire burning. So with great relieve we settled for the night and the following day, with help from George and Mike, we returned to kill sight and even found my pack, which was sold very soon after. So ends our little caribou trip on the Wrangell Mountains and I think was the only caribou that Patrick ever took and I had those little horns on display for many years as it was representative of our few father-son adventures.

Thereafter, I did do some research on the particular rifle that we had and found that it was one that had in fact caused a number of serious injuries and deaths because of this malfunction and involved more than a few legal suits. I don't know where my friend John McCune purchased it but indeed it was a dangerous weapon to behold.

Oysters and Sheep Don't Mix

This episode involves one of the more catastrophic trips that I made in Alaska and I guess the most frustrating part was that I had one of the few grand opportunities to harvest a true trophy sheep and circumstances intervened. I had done some homework on sheep areas on both the north slope and the south slope of the Brooks Range in the Arctic. The north slope being in the Arctic has genetically had sheep that tend to be smaller bodied and smaller horned. After talking to one of the sheep biologists in Fairbanks he suggested that I check out a few drainages in the south slope as conditions have allowed for them to genetically grow larger. Our jumping off place was Bettles which is about 200-miles north of Fairbanks and is a very small community where a number of outfitting organizations work out of often offering float trips on the nearby rivers and air drop-offs into the Gates of the Arctic National-al Park which is again probably 100 more miles northeast of Bettles, all true Artic experiences.

Our neighbors of 28-years, John Tongen, an outstanding gentleman and his wife, Jane, had truly experienced Alaska as John was in the banking business and had worked in a variety of communities including the far north of Barrow, Nome on at least two different job assignments, the Kenai Peninsula, Fairbanks, Anchorage and was in the banking business in Valdez and then years later returned to be the administrative officer for the School District of Valdez. John is a wonderful fellow with long legs and always with much enthusiasm and laughter. I still maintain contact with John and Jane who are currently living in Arizona but do a good deal of traveling. John had minimal experience at sheep hunting and really didn't have much interest al-though I talked him into going with me on this trip to the Arctic. He was in great shape and always was fit. Our plan was to drive to Fairbanks then fly commercially to Bettles and go from there by air taxi that I had made contact with. As noted, Bettles was a small little burg on the banks of the Koyukuk River and I think the population at times is only 10 or 15 people but during the summer it is a tourist hub.

I had been in Bettles on previous occasions, the one notable venture was one up to the famous Anatuvuk Pass which is another 100 miles north and above the Artic circle and is one of the oldest known native villages in the interior Alaska. The Anatuvuk Pass itself has been there for millenniums and is the site of the caribou migration that goes through a narrow valley near the village and is the source of all of their protein and all parts of the animal are used for clothing, etc.. On that particular trip it was a moose venture and it was a successful one although the size of the critter was less than I had hoped as historically there has been some very large moose taken out of that area. Just spending time in Anatuvuk Pass is an experience in itself as you see remnants of old hovels and dugouts that have been used in many years gone by.

The pivotal situation that colored this entire trip began in Fairbanks when we spent the evening with a good friend of mine, Mr. Paul Barrett, who was at the time was a prominent attorney and owned a beautiful home on the Chena River. Down from Paul's home is one of the local restaurants that's situated on the Chena River and is a hotspot for eating and noted for its excellent cuisine. For whatever reason, that evening John and I decided to try some hors d'oeuvres of oysters, which I have never tried before in my life. God knows why I decided this evening to try them and as I remember they weren't particularly good, however that decision cost me dearly. As John and I began our descent into Bettles I could tell that my head and stomach were progressively becoming more uneasy. I seldom if ever have any problems with air-sickness so this was unusual. Upon arrival I could tell that this uneasiness and stomach issue was not going to get any better and it progressed rapidly to the point where I was totally nauseated with extreme stomach cramping. We were scheduled to fly out the following morning to begin our sheep venture but as the day and night progressed I became extraordinarily ill and I can not remember to this day when I have been that impaired. We were situated in a small cabin near the runway with no indoor plumbing and basically two little cots. I can not understate the fact that I thought I was going to die with nausea and stomach issues that were deplorable. I remember almost being unable to stand and dragging myself literally out the door trying to find the outhouse or at times could not make it. This went on continuously through the night and the next morning found me still very queasy and weak. I think this is probably the one and only time I got bona fide food poisoning and there certainly was no medical attention of any sort in the village. After laying about that day, I finally talked myself into trying to make an effort the following morning and off we went. I had done some homework on an area called Our and Your Creek which is almost due east of Bettles crossing the Alaska Pipeline and into the Chandalar River, a tributary that forks as it makes it way out of the Chandalar Lake area. It is a very beautiful area although I couldn't appreciate its beauty as I was still reeling from my sickness. As we did some circling I looked out and to some amazement, in an open pasture-like area were four rams and I couldn't make out their size but they were in a rather idyllic position. We made a spontaneous decision to get dropped off at a near pond area and there began our hunt. As it turned out the climb was relatively easy, probably the easiest one I ever recall in my many sheep ventures. I don't think it took more than two or three hours to reach a level that would be parallel with the sheep that we thought we had located.

As per state regulations one cannot hunt that same day that one flies so we setup our small bivy camp, my two-man tent that is barely large enough to lie down in but it does provide some shelter from the elements. As morning broke we found ourselves in intense fog that was so thick that we that we did not dare to even venture more than several hundred yards from the tent as finding our way back could be a real issue. As I recall, we sat the day and night out hoping for a break in the weather. On the third day, we journeyed out and I found the four sheep that we were looking for and they were very close to the area that we had saw them from the air three days before. Again, for sheep it was very unusual to find them in such an open area and I'm guessing that they had probably been pushed into this area from some hunting pressure as we were into the third week of the season. The stalk went smooth and easy as ever and we had no major rock issues or cliffs to deal with as we approached the sheep from a parallel level and soon found ourselves within a 100-yards of these beautiful animals and to our amazement they were all very large rams. John generously said he didn't care which sheep I took, that I could take the big ram and he would take the one behind, etc.. This was going to be too easy as it generally one finds himself hanging on for dear life and climbing up some God-awful rocky or glacial areas that can make the stalk very demanding. As the shots rang out, I was absolutely astonished that the sheep I was shooting at didn't react and they all bolted except for one that still stood there, obviously hit. I was so dumbfounded that I didn't even put a secondary shell into my gun although I did put the final coup de grace on John's sheep so I can at least say I was party to a 40-inch sheep. The other sheep took off in a wild non-stop flight and there was nothing to slow them up as this open expanse just kept them running.

Usually in other circumstances they would have probably gone up into the rocks and you would have had a secondary chance at them, as they are generally not all that spooky. In this case they had no place to go but straight ahead and we never did find them again. John's sheep was a wonderful trophy with really interesting gnarling of the horns, a beautiful late season cape and truly was a real trophy. My only explanation for my miss was I am almost sure that the barrel of my gun did not clear the rock pile that I was peering over. Often this can occur as your scope sits higher than your barrel and while the scope will show a clear view, the barrel itself could be too close to the rock and this is what I think occurred. Needless to say this could have been an issue if the bullet would ricochet off a rock at that close distance and shatter. However, still to this very day it dumbfounds me and I have never found myself in such a situation with the true opportunity to bring down a large sheep, which of course was always one of my goals. There have been only two other occasions that I've had the chance to take 40-inch sheep or better and in both of these cases there were circumstances that precluded this to my great frustration. Now that I find myself in my decrepit age, sheep hunting is only a daydream as I don't have the legs nor the mental wherewithal to try another sheep venture.

John's sheep was mounted by myself and it still remains in his home in Arizona and I often look at the picture of the hunt and shake my head with circumstances that ensued but so goes the "fickled finger of fate" as my father used to say. I never did go to the doctor although the symptoms persisted for a number of days even after returning from the trip.

There was one other final effort to redeem myself on sheep hunting in the Bettles area and this occurred several years later with the company of another friend, Robert Peca. I'm beginning to think that my stories are so fraught with these kind of disasters that I harken not to put them to print as they certainly read so negative and I truly did have many a good fortune in my trips over the years. However, it seems that the Bettles karma once again jumped out and bit me in another trip that I can relay. On this trip we found ourselves arriving in Bettles and I had been given some scoop from a fellow taxidermist that told me about a neat area close to the Gates of the Artic National Park and one that he had been to several times and he gave me very detailed descriptions of how to hunt to area. We found ourselves in that God-awful little cabin that I was so sick in awaiting the weather to clear sufficient for us to depart. As we sat there pondering our adventure we began checking some of our gear to make sure that we were ready to go.

John Tongen's Big One 40" - Brooks Range

Part of the process was to check our two small white gas stoves and they both lit and seemed to be in good working order. We laid down for a brief nap and as we awoke I nonchalantly went over to where my stove was sitting and picked it up and as I did it almost exploded in my face as it had obviously been in a very low burn state that was not detectable and as I picked it up the gas ignited into a large puff of fire and smoke. The next thing I knew my sleeves and jacket were aflame and Robert instinctively grabbed something and smothered it out.

I had a polypropylene shirt on that is made from synthetic oil product and easily ignites and they always tell you that if you're on an airplane don't wear anything that's polyester as it's very flammable and in this case it surely was. My entire sleeve was burned and the side of my face and hair were singed markedly. I surveyed the damage to my face and arm and while my face was not too bad, my forearm was not so good. It immediately blistered up to a huge bulbous mass that was more than a little alarming. It so happened that the wife of the pilot was a nurse of some sort and she perused my afflicted arm and shook her head with some dismay and told me in no uncertain terms that this was something that needed to be attended to. She strongly recommended that we not fly out with this kind of burn as it could be infected and other more dire circumstances could occur. However, in our stubborn ways and the distance and money already expended I said the hell with it, I'm gonna go anyways! We took off in the direction of the Gates of the Artic and flew at least a good hour or more but as we flew, the pilot kept looking over at me and could see that my arm was becoming increasingly blistered and he became emphatic to the point where he said in all good faith cannot be party to dropping you off in this condition. He said that if the weather would go badly he may not be able to get back and if something would become worse with the burn I could be in a serious situation. We circled for a few moments and finally I reluctantly made the decision to return to Bettles. This was a very expensive mess up and I can only accept the fact that we were not meant to hunt sheep out of Bettles and the karma that I alluded to earlier must truly be in play. It was a very expensive trip and all we got out of it was a 2-hour air flight which was not cheap particularly up in the Artic were the gas prices are extraordinary. In conclusion, I will probably never see Bettles again but I often have memory flashes of these ill-faded ventures. I periodically see documentaries on Bettles and some of the trips that people take out of that area and reminisce about my circumstances.

The Puale Bay Brown Bear Venture • 1980

One of my first brown bear hunts was with my good friend John McCune. I go into some length on my experiences with the McCune clan in later chapters, as truly they were one of the more influential people in my Valdez hunting travels. I had always wanted to go down the Alaskan Peninsula but really didn't know where to begin. The Alaska Peninsula, for those not familiar, is an area that stretches down hundreds of miles eventually trailing into the Aleutian Islands. Some of the largest bears in the world and some of the largest moose and caribou have come from that area over the last many years.

I had an occasion to talk to a local gentleman, named Milford Taylor, who was the principal of the elementary school and had been one of the founding fathers of the Valdez area. I later became good friends with his grandsons and had many a tale with them. Milford had settled in a homestead type of cabin at Mile 10 of Valdez and was a very active in his early days as a guide even as he aged was the preeminent trapper in the area along with his oldest son, Bill. I recall being at his house one day and he had some outrageous movies of some of his guiding experiences down on the peninsula and had spent some time at Puale Bay which is very close to the Katmai National Refuge. So with that in mind, I tried to figure out a way to make a trip down that way and contacted one of the local air services in King Salmon. John was eager to go and had previous experience when he was living in Dillingham before moving with his wife, Debbie to Valdez in the early 70s probably a year or so after we arrived.

We flew approximately 75 to 100-mile trip due south out of King Salmon and with some borrowed equipment including a tent, we were on our way with great expectations. I should note that I had just recently had major surgery on my back and had been significantly crippled up for a number of years so I was literally a month or so out of surgery when this trip occurred. I looked very gaunt and I would guess I only weighed 160-pounds at the time. Upon our arrival, the bay is certainly idyllic in many ways with waterfalls in the background as well as a major tributary that ran into the base of the bay. There were interesting rock formations and rookeries of untold sea birds. The tent, at the time, I think was one of the better ones made and we tried to secure it but soon experienced what the winds on the Alaska Peninsula can do to equipment. They were relentless and the tent swayed and one point within a few days we could tell that the friction on the rain fly on the center pole was actually shredding the fabric. I think we tried to make some make-do repairs with the use of duct tape and it survived the trip and I believe the owner was able to return it to the original manufacturer and did get a replacement. The first three or four days were indeed uneventful. The wind blew and we made a number of short outings, one of which involved a short overnight on the hillside behind the tent but had very few sightings if any. I think somewhere around the fifth day I was nestled in the tent and John came running breathlessly to the campsite saying he had just spotted a brown bear coming off of the ocean and heading inland. It later turned out to be a walrus carcass that the bear was feeding on and he had then decided to return to a safer haven. So it was paramount that we make our way back as quick as possible before the bear was out of reach. This involved us running as best we could and again I was not in the best of shape.

I believe even at one point John was willing and able to actually carry me across a small bit of water that I could not manage because I didn't have the proper footwear on. We made our way to a knoll overlooking the creek bottom that the bear was heading towards and with a lot of flurry John at the last moment handed me his trusty and recently modified .375 magnum gun that had been worked over by his older brother, Randy, and I had never shot that gun and didn't realize the sizeable recoil. So with little thought in mind other than trying to get off a shot, the gun reported and I soon found myself with blood running down my nose as I was scoped by the recoil of the gun.

The good news was the bear collapsed and John had a good laugh as he saw the bloodletting that occurred over my right eyebrow. That bear was not gigantic but was certainly a mature one and had a light brown colored hide and subsequently was mounted life-size and found its way to the Valdez city museum and was displayed there for well over 30-years until other occurrences found it at the local Westmark Hotel. The next couple of days John made several journeys and we had more than one close call as we made a sneak on a bear to the point of getting less than a couple yards and John in his fearless manner wanted to get a close up with his camera. We did well until the bear winded us and then he was fortunately was off in the opposite direction. John had several opportunities but was keen on finding a bear that was larger than the one he had already taken several years previous. So ended our trip to Puale Bay and we came back with at least one critter and some good memories.

As noted, I have multiple other stories about John and his exploits and he made many a trip with his two brothers, Glen and Randy, both sheep hunting and I think they did make a trip to Kodiak Island were Randy was able to get a sizeable bear in the 9-foot range. John and his younger

John McCune at Puale Bay
First Brown Bear, 1980

brother, Glen made several successful sheep hunting trips, one being in the Chitna glacier area where they walked literally into Canada because it was the home of some of the largest sheep in North America. I know that they also had fruitful trip into an area also in the Wrangell Mountains. Other trips I know of included goat hunting trips relatively close to Valdez where they always seemed to succeed in finding "The Big One". There was one other memorable trip that I accompanied John and his brother, Randy on, into the Alaska Range that is now a National Park. The lake we landed on was the famous Twin Lakes were a gentleman had lived for 50-years and had written a remarkable book documenting his years living in the wilderness. The book is called One Man's Wilderness by Sam Keith from the journals and photographs of Richard Proenneke. This is an idyllic area on the far side of the Alaska Range full of valleys and countless miles of tundra and the home of many a great critter both moose and caribou. I had taken my bow and arrow on that venture and lost all of my arrows in a vane effort at stalking and was less than apt in my shooting ability.

I recall one late afternoon when John and Randy spotted a large herd of caribou that seemed to be miles away and they were running in a very erratic manner, stopping momentarily and then running again. We later found out that it was their way of surviving the onslaught of flies and mosquitos that literally driving them wild. In any event both John and Glen decided to make a go for it and left and I did not see them return until sometime well into the night after midnight. John was carrying the entire meat from the caribou which I'm sure was close to 200-pounds and at that point John was more than capable of managing such weight and always did these things with my amazement.

It was sometime after these events that John and Debbie decided to leave Alaska and go to Colorado for a change of pace. Several years later John returned and somehow I was able to rekindle his latent interest in sheep hunting and put his name in for the sheep permit draws that were highly coveted including the Tok Management Area and later on the Delta Management Area. The Tok permit was indeed one of the more coveted one in the state and we somehow managed to come up with permits that year and found ourselves flying into one of the more famous parts of the area, landing on a sheer ridge with the famous 40-Mile Air service who had pioneered this area since 1959 and had built special landing spots for this purpose. Unfortunately, our trip to Tok turned out to be an absolute miserable one. We landed with sunshine and the next day found us climbing to the summit surrounded by many a ram. We decided to cautiously take our time to be sure we picked out the right one before we proceeded. The next morning, however brought us to the bitter realization that we were in a full-out snowstorm and all we could manage to see was blowing snow and the temperatures less than bearable. We spent two nights in this misery and I remember firing up my tiny Primus stove every fifteen to twenty minutes as I lay shivering in our small tent. It reached a point where we could no longer tolerate this madness and we retreated reluctantly down the mountain to our basecamp in hopes that the weather would clear. Several days later we found ourselves trekking back up the mountain again only to find that nothing really had changed and the weather seemed to be getting even colder even though the snow had subsided. The sheep in this particular valley had vanished and we concluded that this was not going to be our day.

The following year we found ourselves also successful in the sheep draw in the adjoining Delta Junction Area, also a coveted area but the sheep for whatever reason did not have the same genetic superiority as those in the Tok Area. John was less than thrilled with the prospects of going on this sheep hunt and remarked that his enthusiasm was waning as he had already taken some very large sheep in his previous ventures, often going by himself.

The one being in the Chitna Glacier areas were he took a truly magnificent animal that was over 43-inches. But once again, John agreed to trek along and we flew into the Delta Area. On that trip we seemed to have walked forever and I could never keep up with John who seemed to be tireless. After five days of fruitless pursuits we returned to an area where John basically said he was going to go until he finds something and I told him to have at it and I would be sitting here waiting when you come back. I recall vividly him heading up a steep ravine and he always made things look so effortless. Many hours later he returned with a fine sheep on his back and this represented his last successful sheep hunt. Unfortunately, the year after was indeed a sad one as John flew out of Valdez with one of the local pilots who turned out to have minimal experience and the tragedy that occurred still shakes the minds and souls of those that knew him so well. At the risk of being too editorial, I always thought that if John had been the pilot of that airplane that things would have turned out differently. John was always one to push the limits of everything he did but was always on the same token able to maintain a measure of control. However, in this case he was at the mercy of the pilot who made some very basic and critical mistakes.

I still maintain contact with John's brothers, both Randy and Glen who are interesting and talented folks for sure. We often commiserate over our experiences with John and the loss and sorrow involved.

The McCune Experience

As I have already acknowledged, if were not for Debbie McCune I probably would not have undertook this effort to recapture some of the experiences of these past 40+ years and talk about some of the great friends that I've met along the way. Debbie went so far as to send me the recorder that I've been using and was instrumental in putting some of the rough drafts to print.

How do you do justice to capture the essence of the McCune clan and their multi-faceted lives? I've had the good fortune of knowing the McCune family in various ways. I don't know exactly what motivated John and Debbie to Valdez but I suspect it was like so many young people who moved there at the time when they were getting ready for the building of the Trans-Alaska Pipeline and everybody was looking for

John McCune - Last Sheep
Delta Junction

the jobs that came with that amazing construction. I think that the total number of cost for building the 800-mile line was somewhere well over two billion dollars. At that time the town boomed from 1,000 people to over 10,000 housing was a significant issue for everybody and the cost of living skyrocketed accordingly. They built a number of very large man camps to provide for the workers that arrived in droves but John and Debbie were capable enough to build their own abode. In fact, I think John ended up building at least three homes in Valdez and did it basically from scratch with the help of Debbie and in between his work hours. The McCune's presented themselves as a dynamic couple for sure. Debbie was cute as a bug and vivaciously effervescent and John on the other hand was more quiet but was the picture of health and prowess and built like a linebacker and I believe he did play ball either in high school or maybe some college ball. His primary interest was almost inclusively that of exploring Alaska, which he began from the very onset. I was always struck by his core strength and his wide shoulders that seems to slope and were begging for a backpack to be suspended.

John's older brother, Randy, spent several years in Valdez working in education but subsequently returned to Michigan. His younger brother, Glen, came up on a few occasions to do some sheep hunting with John and also managed to take a hellacious 50-ft fall off of a cliff that cost him months of rehab. I know the brothers climbed many a mountain including those directly above Valdez where they took several very large mountain goats.

The McCune family originally came from Ohio and ended up in central Michigan. The DNA that seems to run through them all, hovers around capturing the outdoor experience in any way possible. They all pursued artistic enterprises and those were always related with trying to capture mother nature in its glory. Their father, Frank, flew B-17 Fortresses during World War II and I think had many missions over Germany which in those days was one of the precarious positions that one could have. I believe there was somewhere near 200,000 airmen that were lost in those raids. I often thought that some of the risk-taking that some of the boys inherited came from their dad as piloting in those days must have been a horrendous experience. John in particular was always willing to push the envelope in terms of trying hair-raising adventures but always managed to be in full command of all that he endeavored. I know that Glen has done a number of frightening things to do with cave explorations and Randy still spends much of his time in out-of-door activities and taught an outdoor survival skills class in Michigan.

In those early years John and Debbie were indeed busy,

not only building homes but also exploring the Price William Sound on their very nice boat. They seemed to be tireless in their energy and I know John was working "seven-twelves" and every other week he would be on to a work project or heading up to the nearest mountain.

Anytime that I think of John I always I always categorize him as a very special individual and I can only think of one other person that has some of the innate qualities of being in tune with the outdoors. In my journeys with him he was always first to see the critter and self-assured in the best route to take and his motto was always going the extra mile if you really want to find the trophy animal. His climbing skills were effortless it seemed and he could carry God knows how much weight on his back without even slowing him down. One of his most prideful adventures involved taking a tremendous 43-inch ram off the Chitna Glacier. At that time a large poster was developed with him sitting with a quiet smile and truly captured his essence.

I have already covered a number of trips I took with John including the first brown bear that I ever managed and also a grizzly bear that was taken on one of our sheep hunts. Any time I was with John he would always take the lead and would load his gigantic pack with more meat and horns than I could imagine. I was always left picking up the gear and other pieces, as I truly could not have accomplished what he could do seemingly so easy. I recall one trip down on the Alaska Peninsula where a very large bull caribou had died in the middle of a pond and the next thing I knew John was out in the middle of the pond up to his waist in water pulling that entire caribou back to shore. He packed that entire bull caribou in his pack a number of miles through some God-awful tundra, full of tussoks that would always trip you and the footing was poor. All of that weight lifting did take its toll over the years and I know in some of the final trips that he took he had to bandage his knees as they had taken a beating and probably would have had to done some knee replacement at some point along the way. Unfortunately because of circumstances that followed, that never did occur. At the risk of being redundant, I always saw John as one of the most competent outdoorsmen that I've ever known. I would follow him with great faith as I always knew that he would take the right route and had an inherent sense of his surroundings. The one other exception to this to be would be the Wade brothers, namely James Wade who has that same intangible quality of being in tune with his surroundings and always able to make the right moves at the right time and that was coupled with the physicality and know how to accomplish whatever he is pursuing.

In addition to John's hunting prowess he was a great carpenter and did some amazing work in Valdez. The entire Mc-

John McCune - The Bull

Cune clan are indeed artisans and the DNA that runs through them is apparent in all they do including John's son, Ryan who is just recently got into chainsaw carving and is producing some wonderful products. He recently hosted a chainsaw competition in Valdez and this attracted some of the best people in the business from all over the world including Germany and Australia as well as a number of other states. In the brief time that he got into it he is already moving at a rate in which himself could be competitive in his expertise. Both Glen and Randy, back in their Michigan abodes are fully invested in producing wonderful artistic projects. Glen in particular is not only a great painter but he does a considerable amount of sculpting and carving that are truly remarkable. Randy has been doing professional outdoor photography and for many years produced an impressive catalog of some of his finer works. The ranges of skills go from restoring old boats to making fine canoes and God knows what else they have created over the years.

Debbie and John, during their many years in Valdez, were both very active in skiing and it became a family affair with their son Ryan quickly taking up snowboarding which he became very proficient at and is still enthralled with the excitement and participates in some of the "world's extreme" activities that occur every spring in Valdez. I know that Debbie accompanied John on a few adventures and her most coveted one was when she ventured with him on a major sheep hunt involving fourteen hours of vertical climbing and capped it off by making an impressive long-distance shot at a nice dall sheep. I believe Debbie also did a bit of writing on her experiences and was able to do so in a very adept manner in describing her travels in the Wrangell Mountains.

The Eureka Sheep Hunt 1974

The one story that I can interject at this point is one of the very first sheep hunts that I participated in and it was with John in the Eureka Area, midway between Anchorage and Valdez. At the time we secured the services of one of the local air taxi guys whose name eludes me at this point but he charged us all of $150 each to take us approximately 80-miles off the Glenn Highway and dropped us off after we were able to find a large band of sheep in the area. This trip started on Labor Day and at that time we only had a few days to accomplish this feat which was truly not enough time and also it was coupled with the fact that Debbie was well along in her pregnancy with their first child, Ryan. This trip turned out to be a challenge of extraordinary expenditure of energy and fortitude but at

My First Sheep

the time we were both very youthful and I somehow managed to keep up. I know we left on a Friday or Saturday morning giving us only three days to find the sheep and then return to the drop off point on Monday by 3:00. This did not give us much time and we had a considerable walk, I'm guessing at least seven or eight miles before we even got close to the sheep that we had seen. It truly became a marathon as things developed. As it turned out, we were able to successfully scale a relatively high mountain and found ourselves gazing down at a large band of twenty rams or so and we both managed to knock two down and of course, John always got the bigger one but I was happy to at least say that I had taken a dall sheep. This occurred in

Johne McCune, First Sheep

late evening and we did not have time to field dress them but John had the wherewithal to cover his animal with his jacket and I did not do so and returned the following day to find that eagles or crows had neatly stripped the hair from the cape of the sheep that I had taken. This made it unusable for taxidermy purposes. Of course the eagle managed to take the hair from the most critical part of the animal namely along the neck area which rendered it unusable and I was a bit distressed about this. So began the great pack out of both sheep which amounts to somewhere in the neighborhood of at least 75-pounds without gear. Our plan was to pack them out to the air drop off base and then return and pick up our tent and other belongings. As we started our return trip along the little Nelchina River we noticed something rather peculiar on the hillside above us. As it turned out, it was the four legs of a grizzly bear that was laying on his back and flailing them in the air for whatever purpose. Our first assumption was that maybe it was a sow nursing some cubs which would not be a good

Johne McCune, A Few Days Later

situation in any manner so we dropped our packs and made a circumvent of the situation and found ourselves above the bear to fully evaluate what was going on. The bear had dug a sizeable hole, maybe just for the coolness and we could not make out any cubs. As the bear finally decided to get up my old .06 reported and now we were stuck with what to do in retrieving this bear from miles away. The bear turned out to be a relatively old female squaring probably in the 7.5 to 8-foot range and unfortunately the skull got lost when I was having it prepared. In any event, the hide itself weighed in the neighborhood of 100-pounds with the head and feet adding to the already burdensome task that we were dealing with. I believe we left the bear skinned and in a pile continued our trek back to the air drop base with our sheep staying only to unload our packs and then start the return trip that same night. That trip back was an eternity and I remember my legs being so wobbly that I didn't know if I could continue. At times it seemed to be an impossible task but I think with the good fortune of having a full moon we were able to struggle back to our original campsite. The next morning found us staggering to our feet and beginning again the return trip, this now coupled with carrying the bear hide out and I'm almost positive that John probably did the bulk of that challenge. Miraculously we stumbled our way back

The Eureka Bear – Very Old

and arrived within minutes of when the air taxi returned and then it was back to Valdez another 250-mile trip so truly we packed a lot of adventure into those three days and made it back in time for the birth of Ryan so it was one of those memorable outings that I thought worthy of trying to recapture in this journal.

Judy the "Raffle Queen"

Anyone who has taken time to fumble through these pages may have realized that there was little mention of the role of my lovely and patient wife, Judy. While Judy has never had any interest or passion for the out-of-door things she has always been there for me and never complained and in fact encouraged and supported my endeavors however crazy or expensive they were. If she complained she did it quietly and basically let me do my thing despite I'm sure that she had misgivings at times about what I was getting myself into.

Judy, on the other hand, as anyone who knows her has spent most of her life doing for others. This is somewhat reminiscent in who in her own quite way was the "ear" for many a soul in her years and she seemed to attract people who would spend hours telling her their problems. She found us a home in Valdez that which as we arrived was a very small burg but grew exponentially as the various booms occurred with the pipeline construction and then the horrendous influx of people during the 1989 oil spill. She poured her heart out in all manners of volunteerism and I know had a pile of trophies and acknowledgements including the "First Lady's Volunteer Award of Alaska". She was co-chair for years of the infamous Gold Rush Celebrations that at one time lasted for several weeks during the summer and was the highlight of the year. Even as recently as this past year she participated in organizing various aspects of that gala activity. At some point along those many years she took great pleasure in selling raffle tickets for almost any and every organization in town. I would harken to say she raised hundreds of thousands of dollars for various agencies and causes. Everybody in town knows Judy and she still maintains contact with many of her old friends. She soon became know as the "Raffle Queen" and people would often duck when they saw her coming as they knew they would have to dig deep into their pockets to buy what Judy was selling. In almost every case she was successful in exploiting their generosity she took great delight in the interactions that she had with so many people.

Over and above that she became part of the fabric of

Queen for a Day - Gold Rush

the lives of many families in our little town of Valdez. Every funeral, wedding, christening, birthday, potluck or any social grouping she was usually involved and looking out for other people's needs and interests. There was a time she used to dress up as a clown and showed up at kid's birthday parties and had a special knack for being there for others in need and in fun. Leaving Valdez during the past few years as been indeed a difficult transition and I often regret making that decision as it truly took away from what was most important to her. Even living in Wyoming as we do at the moment she maintains contact with the local Valdez activities and still participates to a certain degree from afar. Our travels as previously noted involved moving to Canada during my graduate school years, returning to Minneapolis and then on to Alaska in 1972. For a number of years we returned to the states to be closer to our parents and this involved several moves, one to North Dakota and one to Billings, Montana. In 2004 we found ourselves returning to Valdez and spent ten years there as if we had never left.

On the downside of things I thought it would have always been nice to enjoy some of the many experiences that I've had in the outdoors but I soon realized that it was not her cup of tea. I suspect that her great enthusiasm for volunteerism is probably from the fact that I did not provide the amount of attention and acknowledgement that dear old husbands should. I could probably get a bit analytic at this point but would probably not be wise but do share some guilt on the fact that I spent maybe too much time away from home doing my own thing and not being attentive to the family and its needs. Judy has always been a backup for me as I have aged she seems to have taken up the slack doing things that I am not comfortable with and she has been more than generous in putting up with all of my foibles and personal shortcomings which I am acutely aware of. Whether we return to Valdez or Alaska is something that haunts me daily and I am trying to balance the reality of the aging process and the cost and finances involved in living in Alaska, specifically Valdez. I know for Judy's sake it would be wonderful to get back into her comfort zone again and I'm sure very easily resume activities and engagement with old and new friends.

It would be easy to say that I could probably fill a book with testimonials from people who have had contact with Judy over the years as she has been the best of friends to many and has often done so much for others. Moving has been difficult indeed although she has made some friends recently and is trying to recreate to some degree some of the activities that she has been involved with in Alaska. In true Judy fashion, she was the driving force behind establishing a new and very popular dog park in Wyoming, which aptly earned her the nickname of "The Hammer" given to her by friends because she perseveres and accomplishes great things when others may have given up.

I reflect back on what Judy had to put up with as we went through the many years together. Early reflections recall me boiling skulls in the kitchen of our small apartment in Alaska and God knows she put up with more blood and guts in her kitchen sink than most women would tolerate. The house was always adorned with creatures and at one point in our first home in Valdez I think every wall had something dead of some sort hanging there and I'm sure it did grate on her but she seldom complained.

In recent times Judy has accompanied me on a few trips to Canada and with age I have found that my confidence to manage the traffic has become more difficult. I don't know what the next step will be, if we will continue in Wyoming or explore some other community.

Of Family, Kids and Dogs

Judy and I have been blessed with three healthy and bright children, all of which have now grown and gone their separate ways. They all have been successful to one degree or another and have received good educations and two of them went on to get graduate degrees. As a father I guess I always thought it would have been neat to have passed on some of my passions of the out-of-doors to my children but this was not the case and they all picked their own directions and interests as it should be. In those early years when we were young parents, I'm fully aware that I probably was not particularly giving, this being a reflection of my immaturity. The kids early on though were able to find interests and had the motivation to pursue them.

My youngest son, Patrick, did accompany me on a number of trips that I've already spoken about to some degree and in his early teen years made many a trip to our local lake to bird hunt. Our oldest, Angela, was a very genteel young woman and had no interest in my craziness but was very successful in her school years, was on the national honor society and participated in a number of high school sports including basketball, cheerleading, etc.. Angela was the apple of the eye of my parents, representing the first grandchild and spent a good deal of time in her growing up years going back and forth to Minneapolis. She was a beautiful girl and I harken to say she was the perfect child and represents the most conservative of the trio of siblings. Southern California drew her attention however she did attend a year at Seattle University and I think was drawn to the sunny environ of California were she attended the University at Fullerton State. She has always been a sunshine girl and finds herself now in Anchorage with her husband, Tony. She graduated with a degree in Advertising and worked in a number of organizations primarily in the real estate business but also in other arenas and most currently is in an administrative position with the City of Anchorage in their convention and tourism department.

All of our kids returned to Valdez during the summers to make college money and we certainly we were blessed

Tim at Everest Base Camp

Mom, Krista and Judy

with being in Valdez for that purpose as the money at that time was extraordinary, particularly during the oil spill years where jobs were aplenty and all the kids benefited from the great incomes they were able to make for their three months at home during the summers. Timothy, our oldest boy soon found his niche in sports and it seems as young as age 10 or younger he took off on his basketball career where he excelled through high school. He did extremely well in school as did the other children and soon found himself a scholarship and later attended graduate school in France and then Germany. The one factor that I think may have influenced all of them in a positive way was the remote location of Valdez, which allowed them trips to explore other communities in Alaska. The most remarkable being their trips to Barrow, the farthest northern city in North America, where they competed against the Eskimo kids. The journeys to Barrow were also an adventure and I can only think that these kinds of trips provided the groundwork for their willingness to take chances and explore the world beyond the little town of Valdez. I guess if I was to speak to any legacy or inspiration it would have been the fact that I had the good fortune to make many a trip abroad and this could have been a catalyst for the adventures that the boys took, Timmy spending several years in Europe and now finds himself in a global position as in executive on the East Coast. Patrick decided to head west and get as far away from the snow and cold of Alaska where he attended the University of Hawaii beginning with his undergraduate program in a private school and then on to acquiring a graduate degree. His interest has always been in Asia and he's made many a trip to that part of the world. Truly the lifestyle in Hawaii is considerable different than what one finds in Alaska although interestingly we have had a number of people that have been born and raised in Hawaii and living in Alaska, primarily I'm sure for the financial gains as Hawaii is notably known for its low wages. Timmy's travels, even in recent years have been remarkable and even a year or two ago he found himself at the basecamp of Mount Everest and along with his running group has done untold marathons and made quite a number of other adventures around the world.

Krista, our oldest granddaughter probably has shown more interest in my outings than most and during her early years spent most of her summers and vacations at our home. She followed me around on many an occasion, particularly during my trapping days where she trudged faithfully behind me in her snowshoes and seemed to enjoy that experience. I have already detailed her great bear hunt that remains keenly tucked away in my memory bank and one that I know she still has fond memories of.

Tim and Little Timmy

The Whole Clan!

She has made many remarks of how these experiences did influence her life and that has been very gratifying.

This discussion of the kids coming and going in the family gives rise to our reflection on my four-legged friends that have dominated these past many years. As the kids have left, I seemed to be more consumed with my dogs, which have become an integral part of my day-to-day, particularly during retirement. They dominate my days and I can say with some degree of confidence that I have been blessed with some wonderful canines, particularly during

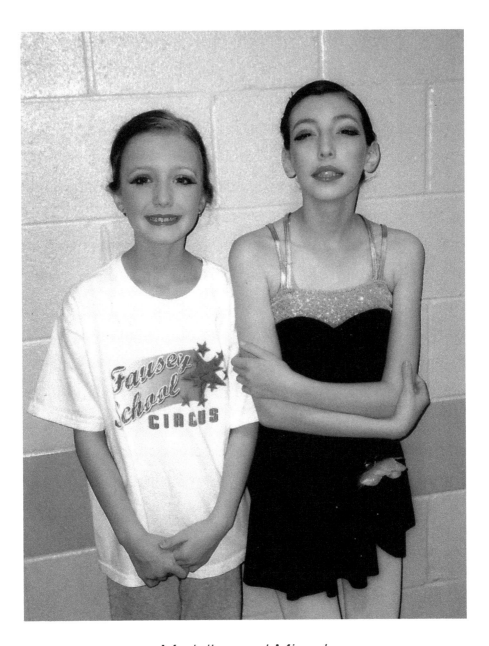

Madeline and Micaela
Serious Ballet Training

the last thirty years or so. My first springer spaniel was attained at age 10 and I still remember that dog's demise, which unfortunately was a very painful circumstance with a very inattentive veterinarian at the time. I did have several other dogs but work and other responsibilities did not allow me to attend to them, one being a weimaraner in Duluth, which remains to be one of the dumbest dogs that I have had to deal with. My dear daughter, Angela, acquired through some suspicious circumstances a very cute little dog name named Richter that was a menace and while she loved it dearly it became so problematic that is disappeared under mysterious conditions. However, as noted, these last 30-years or more have been indulged with four spaniels, one being Dame, a Boykin Spaniel that was at the time a bit of an elitist breed that came out of South Carolina and became that State's dog. At the time of her acquisition there were less than 1500 in the country and Dame was a wonderful companion that I took on many a venture, particularly trips to Minneapolis and hunting in states including Iowa, Washington, South Dakota, etc. She was a strange little spaniel of short stature and great heart and she accompanied me on many a trip to our local duck hunting lake. I devoted at least one story about her that was published in *Alaska Magazine*. I always regretted not having her bred a second time for the chance at an

*Dame - published in **Alaska Magazine***

additional puppy but as the only other male dog available was the dog owned by the judge who was trying the famous Exxon Valdez trial of Captain Joe Hazelwood. It was during the judge's court time that the dog became unavailable and we could not coordinate the timeframes needed and she became too old for further breeding. Soon after the loss of my little friend Dame I acquired a wonderful springer that arrived on one Christmas Eve in the late 80s on our doorstep with our dear friend John McCune and his wife. Q.T. was a dog that with us for over 14 years and accompanied me on many a journey including all of my trapping trips and ventures to the Dakotas, etc. She came from great lineage and was a field bred springer that had a pedigree that came from a very notable field bred champion. From that point forward, I decided that it would only be a field bred springer that I would be interested in. After Q.T. came another wonderful dog that I called Sara (The Lady of Saratoga Trail). She was acquired from a breeder in Illinois that specialized in breading large and long-legged springers and this is what I needed given our snow conditions in Alaska. She again, was as wonderful and as functional a dog as anyone would ever want. I estimated

The bond between hunter and dog, duck and marsh is an age-old tie that binds the seasons.

that she spent over 300,000 miles in my suburban as I got her about the same time I got my 2002 suburban and she was with me almost every mile of the way. I'm guessing she went down the Alaskan Highway with me more than a half a dozen times and I could renumerate some of the interesting confrontations that she had with bears, lynx, wolves and moose but she was there by at my side at ever moment and remained strong up into age 14 and beyond. She recently left me in September of 2018 but remained one of the most faithful and genteel dogs that I have ever known. My most recent springer is a very similar breed and in fact there is some relationship between her and Sara as the original breeder had some lineage that went onto the breeder that I acquired Fergie from. Fergie has turned out to be a dynamo of strength and agility with great instincts and she is probably the most athletic dog that I have ever owned. One has to ponder whether this will be my last dog or whether in fact she will out-live me but these are thoughts I try not to dwell on. As I have aged I have always tended to be a loner, these canines have truly filled in a gap in my day-to-day activities.

I often introspectively ponder if I had been as attentive to the kids as I have been to my dogs that maybe something would have been different, but who knows. As I go through my voluminous albums the number of photos of dogs certainly outweigh the photos of any human sort and I think that is a rather sad commentary in some ways of my pervasive life-style interests.

While Judy never shared the passion for the outdoors stuff as I have over the years she nonetheless was most accepting and supporting of all of the crazy things that I undertook. She put up with the skulls of critters being boiled in her kitchen and all manner of dead creatures hanging from the walls to the point of the absurd. People would often comment on how can you live in a house with all of these dead things and she just accepted it in her benign way. I'm also very cognizant that some of the geographical moves that we made were extremely difficult for her particularly the two times we left Alaska as she had totally invested herself in that community and had provided help and support to God knows how many volunteer projects. Valdez will always be her home and to some great extent it will also be seen as my home. If I'm not mistaken she already has a cemetery vault sitting and waiting for me at the local cemetery so that in all likelihood could be my final resting place near the Robe River where I spent hundreds of days plundering about and in fact, two of my favorite dogs are buried in the nearby area.

Judy approached everything she did with a spirit of altruism and did everything to help make people's lives a little better, including mine. She still remains probably one of the most recognizable people in Valdez despite the fact that time and distance has taken its toll, however she still remains close with a number of people and participates from afar in some of the activities that occur in the community particularly the annual Gold Rush celebration. As we find ourselves sitting in Powell, Wyoming as of this writing I struggle on a daily basis with the folly of my decision to move away from Valdez. However, I reached a point where I had to find some balance between financial survival and the reality of aging and medical concerns. Seeking medical help in Valdez is indeed a challenge, often requiring long trips to Anchorage and the air fare now has almost doubled in cost. The long-term care situation is abominable and approaches the thirty thousand dollar a month, which is absolutely absurd to think that the federal government is reimbursing for that level of care. All of these things have factored into my decision to go down the Alaska Highway one more time and returning could be a real struggle given the fact that the fixed income does not allow for the non-stop cost of living increases that continue to grow exponentially from year to year. In our recent trip to Valdez in the summer of 2018 those expenses were apparent and unfortunately the town had become even more expensive as the monopolies were evident in everything that one would need to survive the day-to-day existence. Nonetheless, it's where our hearts lie and if I could magically change our decision, I probably would have leased our home and given myself some time to reconcile that decision. However, we will remain in a bit of a quandary until such time that life circumstances take us in one direction or another. Our children are scattered from coast-to-coast and there is no easy solution but I am thankful for having children who are global in their interests and have taken them in directions both east and west.

In recent times, Judy has been generous to accompany me on a few local trips mostly into Canada. As I have found that some of my adventuresome confidence has slipped a bit and making trips of any distance requires some support. So I would like to thank her for her willingness to persist with my interests.

Judy has always been driven by a different passion than I and her need for socialization is evident in all that she does. She has engaged herself in some local activities here in Wyoming and finds that rewarding as she has always been committed to volunteerism wherever it might raise its head.

As I have previously mentioned I had hoped that I had passed on some of my passion for the outdoors onto my children but for the most part they have sought out other interests. I want to thank them for putting up with me in those early years when I was away from home so often. My legacy is likely a spirit of adventure because their travels have certainly opened up worlds of interest that may not have otherwise occurred. I suspect if we would have never left the lower '48' in the early days that their lives probably would have turned out much differently but their world view has been expanded and from that I hope that they have gained a better understanding of the world that we find ourselves in.

As we have reached the autumn of our lives the tendency is of course to always look back and to reflect about what could have been or what should have been different. I guess everybody reaches that same place in time, however some people seem to accept it more graciously than I do. New adventures become more difficult so pondering about what has been seems to be the easiest course of action. I have found myself thinking more so of my parentage, particularly my dear Father who I wish I had had more time with but as things developed I had chosen to move away during those critical last years of his life and often thought that I should have been there to provide a better level of support. I regret never sitting down and listening to some of his philosophizing and I was not too open to some of that thinking and now I regret not taking the time and patience to have immersed myself in the knowledge that he had accrued. He was self-educated and has spent much time imbuing himself with the philosophies of some of the famous theologians including St. Augustan, St. Thomas and his favorite, Descartes. In any event, my dad was ahead of his times in that sense as while he worked in rather mundane positions his thinking was much more sophisticated than most of the people that he came into contact with. I would have relished the opportunity to have captured his thoughts about World War II and the arduous times that he found himself in. Why I didn't take time to capture his words on tape is beyond me. He could have filled up a book with his memoirs regarding the depression years and the war years. What he did create in me was an appreciation for all things out-of-doors, particularly the solitude found in fishing and in quiet walks in the neighboring woods. Fishing in particular was his passion and he did so all the way up to shortly before his death in 1980. I would guess that those early experiences fishing with him in the mornings and our few hunting treks in western Minnesota fueled the passion that I pursued throughout my life. I can also connect with the fact that being an only child creates an environment where one tends to do things by yourself and I always had difficulties functioning in groups and still do. To this day

I will not get myself involved in group hunts beyond one or two companions. I know my father tried to infuse some of these values of communing with nature and that these are the places that he found peace and tranquility. I know that my trapping days still reflect that philosophy and I am most content being myself in a quiet place.

At the risk of going out on a tangent I find abhorrent the technology that is seen in the field of hunting these days and for that matter, the fishing with radar and large boats and mania that seems to go with it is appalling in my mind's eye. Those quiet early mornings on bass ponds were always a mystical experience and I can still see my father grumbling when his quiet repose was interrupted with noisy boats and yacking people. The technology and commercialization of hunting is detestable and it has certainly detracted from the experience and I see on TV the hyped up characters that pound fists and celebrate over kills made at a thousand yards and or harvesting animals taken from box blinds over feeders all of which is not part of what I learned in my growing up years.

I must mention the great patience and love of my mother, who was always there for me and spent the last five years of her life at our home. Again, I don't know why I did not have her talk about those years of the Depression and during the war when she took care of me with very little help and the few meager dollars that were provided by the U.S. Government. I always thought it would be neat to have heard the exhilaration and excitement that she must have felt when my father returned after the war. I know that during the war that he had written many letters and I remember seeing them carefully bound in her cedar chest. They somehow mysteriously disappeared and I assume that was her way of protecting her privacy but I would have loved to have read some of those reflections as they were both very lonely during those difficult years. So it is with this that I bid ado and hope that I have captured some of these more interesting and salient reflections of my experiences.

Angela with Dame & QT

Dame's Poem

October 1995

As sleepy hand reaches out the bed
To stroke that kind and gentle head
She's not there…

Hunter's garb with boots and stride
For sure to bring animated
Excitement to rise –
And, she's not there…

As snowshoes tread on wintry day –
A glance behind, who's following
My way
And, she's not there…

Door ajar – a rush to greet –
With wiggly delight, a friend
To meet –
And, she's not there…

Evening solitude – on sofa rent –
She sits beside with gaze content
And, she's not there…

Nighttime rituals – ice cream
Treats – sadder moments of
Evening replete –
And, she's not there…

Fourteen years of constant
Routine – of misplaced emotion
And loyalty keen –
And, she's not here...

And now a reflection, a
Measure of time – A passing
Generation that's never too kind
And, she's not here...

Goodbye my little brown friend –
I'll think of you often –
As I walk through the woods
Near your river bend's coffin –
And, you'll not be there...

We'll pass by your new space –
My new friend and I
For sure to salve
But never replace...

Where to Bury a Dog

By Ben Hur Lampman, *Gun Dog Magazine*

article originally published in September 1981

A subscriber of the Ontario Argus has written to the editor asking, "Where shall I bury my dog?" It is asked in advance of death.

We would say to the Ontario man that there are various places in which a dog may be buried. We are thinking now of a setter, whose coat was flame in the sunshine, and who, so far as we are aware, never entertained a mean or an unworthy thought. This setter is buried beneath a cherry tree, under four feet of garden loam, and at its proper season the cherry strews petals on the green lawn of his grave. Beneath a cherry tree, or an apple, or any flowering shrub of the garden, is an excellent place to bury a good dog. Beneath such trees, such shrubs he slept in the drowsy summer, or gnawed at a flavorous bone, or lifted head to challenge some strange intruder. These are good places, in life or in death. Yet it is a small matter. For if the dogs be well remembered, if sometimes he leaps through your dreams actual as in life, eyes kindling, laughing, begging, it matters not at all where that dogs sleeps. One a hill, where the wind is unrebuked and the trees are roaring, or beside a stream he knew in puppyhood, or somewhere in the flatness of a pasture land, where most exhilarating cattle graze. It is all one to the dogs, and all one to you, and nothing is lost – if memory lives. But there is one best place to bury a dog.

If you bury him in his spot, he will come to you when you call – come to you over the grim, dim frontiers of death, and down the well-remembered path, and to your side again. And though you call a dozen living dogs to heel they shall not growl at him, nor resent his coming for he belongs there. People may scoff at your, who see no lightest blade of grass bent by his footfall, who hear no whimper, people who may never really have had a dog. Smile at them for you shall know something that is hidden from them, and which is well worth the knowing. The one best place to bury a good dog is in the heart of his master.

Patrick, Natalie & Precious Londo

Krista, Victor, Felgona, Joelle and Jude Ochieng

The following represents the last poem from my father before his death – he wrote many...

> *Podunk*
> *March, 1980*
> *SNOWING.*

For my favorite grandchildren:

WINTER WEARY.

Drabby houses, factory smoke imprisoned under
pewter sky.
Sepia dawn, listless sun, dingy snow, a muffled passerby.
> *Winter weary.*

Months passing with measured tread with no account
of time.
Pleasurable moments seem commonplace, distorted
without rhyme.
> *Winter weary.*

Insane gusts of winter fury rail and buffet about
the house.
Outside the window winnowed drifts sanctuary
for lonely mouse.
> *Winter weary.*

Mad March zephers announce in passing of
grander hopes.
Of runnings rills, a patch of bare, uplifted now to cope.
                    With winter weary.

Ebullient Spring, a screeing red-wing on bended reed.
Pugnacious robin, reluctant worm, burst bud, new seed.
                    Come Spring.

Languid summer, dappled shadows neath breezed leaves.
Molten sun, seared weed, carefree hours,
winter reprieve.
                    Autumn prelude.

Rustling corn, flocked wings, wedged geese clamor.
Enflamed tree, meadow sere, Nature with envied glamour.
                    Melancholy.

Joy, sorrow compartments share for leaves must fall,
Then all is said who wants to be the very last of all?
                    Autumn won't be denied.

Love, Pop.

Angela and Tony Arturo

*Micaela, Pat, Judy
and Timmy*

*Micaela, Timmy,
Tim and Madeline*

The March of the Bulls

In perusing some of the materials that I have produced all of them seem to have a preoccupation with some of the disastrous events that occurred, but of course, those are the ones that you always remember. I was truly blessed to have had a number of very successful ventures one of which involved hunting caribou in the Dillingham area and I had made a number of successful trips there both out of Lake Iliamna and Dillingham. The Mulchatna herd was considered to be one of the largest herds in the state and produced some of the finer trophies. Interestingly, this herd has somehow disappeared after being in this traditional area after God knows how many years and my last communication in that area indicates that the herd may have somehow joined up with one of the central Artic

B&C Bull out of Dillingham 1996 - Career Best

herds. There have been a number of these kinds of anom-
alies with the caribou and biologists are hard-pressed to
explain how after millenniums of trudging the same routes
that they have now either moved on or joined up with oth-

er herds. In any event, I had a number of very successful hunts both again out of Iliamna and Dillingham. Specifically an air service called "Bay Air" out of Dillingham was my most productive resource. A delightful couple ran that business, his name being Tom Schlagel, and they ran a very efficient operation. On at least three occasions I flew friends and acquaintances to an area north of Dillingham near the village of Koliganek. He had a very neat operation where he would use a fixed wing airplane that could take major loads then we would land in Koliganek where he had a gentlemen that was what they call a Super Cub driver. The Super Cub being the workhorse of bush Alaska and its ability to land in small places and take off in a very short distance is incredibly important in bush flying.

Of particular note was a trip I took with a gentleman named Steve Merriam who was the general manager of the telephone company and was an avid archery connoisseur. He was a traditionalist and used a recurve bow with traditional feather fletched arrows and took pride in not getting into the fancy equipment that is now being used. On this trip he not only brought his trusty Black Widow bow but also a rifle, which turned out was his last recourse. We landed near two little ponds and set up a comfortable camp. It seems that maybe on the following day all of a sudden we started seeing herds of caribou and in this instance they were all bachelor bulls in what I believe was a pre-rut phenomenon as they made their way down from the higher elevations to join up with the herds in the area. I don't remember ever having that good fortune as literally every animal that we saw was a bull and in most cases they were very large and indeed impressive. There were strings of them that seemed to go on for several days and we struck by our great fortune. It was during those first few days that I took two extremely large caribou, the largest in my career and was living the great life. Steve made more than a few aborted efforts at getting close with his bow but in each case, at the last moment, things did not materialize and he was unable to get away a close shot which is required with archery equipment, especially traditional gear. At the twelfth hour, Steve reluctantly took a magnificent large caribou and there we were with three very impressive animals all of which I have mounted and unfortunately some have been given away and certainly as of this writing I don't know if Steve still has the one I did for him. This represents one of the high points of my caribou hunts and one that I remember vividly. I don't re-call ever having seen that many trophy quality bulls at one time so that's what makes it such a unique memory.

B&C Bull out of Dillingham 1996

Elk Hunting on Raspberry Island / Kodiak, Alaska

Sometime during the late 80s or early 90s, Steve Goudro, a great friend of mine, and I both successful in drawing elk tags for the Raspberry Island elk herd, an island that adjoins the larger Kodiak Island. These animals were transplanted many years ago and they are Roosevelt elk that were brought up from Oregon or Washington state and have flourished on the islands. Their body size is considerable larger than the Rocky Mountain elk, however their horn grows in configurations that are much different. On Raspberry and several other islands the horn compositions are not particularly impressive as I think it is a matter of genetics and too much cross breeding to produce trophy quality antlers. However, for the most part it is the meat that everyone is pursuing and I also was hopeful that

I would have an opportunity at seeing a Kodiak bear and had purchased a tag for that purpose. The Raspberry Island trip was fraught with a number of gut-wrenching weather conditions. We landed on the southwest side of the island on an inland bay, which I believe was called Onion Bay, and we set up our camp accordingly. We brought a small raft along for the purpose of being able to cover some area and we also spotted some elk as we arrived at our destination. From that point forward things deteriorated primarily because of the weather conditions that are so notorious in that part of the world. The wind and rain of Kodiak are legendary and we indeed found ourselves in the throes of it. Our first effort involved taking the raft several miles down the bay and making a jaunt up to higher elevations to spend a night or two in a bivy type of camp. However, the rains and winds literally forced us off of the hill and we found ourselves stumbling down through the alders only to find that our little raft was upside down and full of water. Getting the motor started and reorganizing our gear was a struggle and we found ourselves bobbing along the shore trying to return to our basecamp. We were totally drenched and we were looking forward to some warmth and dry clothes. As we arrived at our camp we were overcome with dread as we saw that the tent has collapsed and was entirely full of water with backup sleeping bags floating about and everything was a mess to say the least. This presented a rather dangerous situation as getting wet and not being able to dry off can result in some serious consequences. Fortunately, we had the wherewithal to reorganize the tent, dumping it out and putting in on a safer part of the beach. If it was not for the Coleman lantern we would probably never would have dried off. We kept that lantern burning non-stop for at least two days with our stockings and all manner of clothes hanging from makeshift clotheslines within the tent. Slowly but surely we were able to dry off a fair amount of gear but the sleeping bags were another story. Fortunately, we had brought a number of large black plastic bags and we concocted an alternative to putting our feet into a wet bag by putting a plastic bag inside the sleeping bag as well as having one on the outside. This at least gained us some measure of warmth but was not very comfortable for sure.

Across the bay we had noticed another camp and it soon became apparent that they were Coast Guard fellows as Kodiak has one of the largest Coast Guard units in the country. At least on several occasions a large helicopter would arrive with, we would guess, gear and provisions. The noise of that large helicopter surely spooked every elk in the country for miles away. Needless to say it is highly illegal to use a helicopter in any manor in Alaska particularly military equipment, which I guess we could have made a stink about but we chose not to. What was most dismaying however was that any elk that we had previously spotted would surely be miles away and this did not set well with us for sure. I am sure that in the many years that the military has been in Alaska that federal equipment has been misused and I have some first-hand information about that as I was told that meat, etc. and gear was being transported to and from Anchorage to various areas for military personnel. The other compounding issue that effected our success was my beleaguered back which at that time was extraordinarily painful and subsequently had to have some surgery. It made it extremely difficult to make long treks but we did find ourselves stumbling up an adjacent hillside and as I remember Steve took a very nice Sitka black-tailed buck.

At the time, our youth and naivety seemed to have made the trip bearable and Steve in his good nature always found humor in these predicaments. As we were hunkered down in our tent for a number of days, we took the playing cards that we had brought along and strung them neatly along a line trying to dry them out so we could entertain ourselves.

I know we made at least one more attempt at getting up to the high country as we knew the elk were above

*Steve Goudreau smiling after a miserable night
1979*

the tree line and I think it was on one of the final days we found ourselves face-to-face with three very large brown bears. I had purchased a tag for that purpose and could not distinguish one bear from the other although I suspect it was a mother bear and two fully-grown cubs that were in the 8-foot range. At some point I decided to have a go at it and as I lifted my old Browning rifle to my shoulder, fate intervened and the scope was completely fogged in. This often occurs with older model scopes as they are filled with nitrogen to keep them dry. The scope was fogged to the point where I had no vision of the bears and it put us in a rather precarious position as they were quite close. Our only recourse was to retreat down the hill and the bears sauntered off. That probably remains one of my few opportunities to have taken a Kodiak brown bear although I had made one other effort years later near the cabin that he owned on Kodiak Island itself. We struggled through the remaining days watching for our pickup and that trip probably remains one of our most miserable experiences. Steve remembered the occasion with a cute little poem that he gave me at Christmas that is stapled to the wall in my shop.

The final scenario that capped this miserable trip off was a situation that we found ourselves in at the Kodiak airport. In our flurry to gather our gear and load it into the waiting airplane somehow a bit of contraband ended up in my pockets unbeknownst to me and while we were going through security Steve found himself in an argument with security over having ammunition in his pocket. At that time Steve was not going to take no for an answer and some of the interaction became a little more vocal to the point were the security gentleman told us to empty all of our pockets on the counter. It was at that particular moment that I felt the item in question that could have got us in some dire straits and I found myself palming that from hand to hand as I unloaded my pockets and fortunately was able to fool the gentleman. I could feel the blood running cold in my system as I realized the consequences of even this minor infraction given our positions with the state and the Alyeska Pipeline Company. I could visualize having the local gendarmes show up to inspect anything that looked less than legal and the ramifications could have been nightmarish. Stevie still chuckles about this and while I was sweating bullets he was nonchalantly sauntering out of the airport with a whistle and a wink.

The final insult to the trip involved having one of our friends, George Maykowsky and Judge John Bosshard showing up in the middle of the night at our homes making phony elk noises and laughing themselves sick at hearing of our wonderful trip to Raspberry Island. In any event, they enjoyed themselves although I was in no mood to be berated given what we had just survived.

Caught With Our Pants Down

This is a South Dakota story involving very good friends of ours, acquaintances of many years, Herb and Cindy Weichert. They arrived in Valdez about the same time that we did in the early 70s and had two children which I think we are God parents too although I've not played a very active role in the their lives. Herb was a hunk of a guy who was born on a farm in Austin, Minnesota and had been a roofer, working hard his whole life on the family farm. A very jovial fellow with a deep resonating voice and he was always busy doing projects and was quite an accomplished carpenter. He worked in Valdez as the maintenance department director of snow removal. Cindy worked at the Harborview complex and we had certainly a lot of contact over the years and remained close to them, however, Herb passed away several years ago, which remains a source of great sadness.

Herb and I did a number of things while in Valdez, mostly taking waterfowl trips around the area, however the one story that bears repeating had to do with a trip to South Dakota. At the time Herb had two great looking golden retrievers and of course I had my springer spaniel, Q.T.. Herb would periodically check on his home in Austin and I at the same time I would be checking on my mother in Minneapolis and we decided to get together and make a trip to central South Dakota near the town of Platte. I had been out to the Kott residence before and we had a num-

ber of very successful hunts prior to this trip as the birds were plentiful and we were young and vigorous enough to cover a lot of miles. I recently stopped at the Kott Farm not many years ago and things have changed dramatically with the loss of C.R.P. Land, which had diminished the cover that they pheasants require for survival.

This particular year that Herb and I made this trip there was a bonanza of birds and I think we ended up getting our full complement of our limits. It was at a time when the weather was wicked with snow on the ground and cold November winds blowing.

At some point in the hunting days that we were there I told Herb that I was looking for an old wagon wheel to mount some pheasants on as a display piece and it so happened that an abandoned farm was close to where we were hunting although we were somewhat skeptical that it was on the Kott Farm property. However, this did not deter us from checking out the abandoned property and I think with some persistence Herb agreed to help me find a wheel in the pile of debris that seemed to surround the old barns. I'm sure that down deep Herb's conscience must have been somewhat touched as he knew the rules of private property in rural areas. The amount of no trespassing and no hunting signs are everywhere these days it seems and I guess one cannot blame the poor farmer from protecting his property from strangers. In any event, as we stumbled our way through the abandoned farm there was an old wagon with a wheel still attached, part of which was under the snow and as noted, the wind was howling and it was extremely cold. Herb with his mechanical wisdom decided that he could somehow figure out how to get that wheel off the wagon and was bent over down on his knees trying to extricate that wheel. I stood there hovering over him and I'm not sure what I was doing except maybe providing some words of encouragement. It should be noted that Herb had a serious hearing deficit and one had to speak quite loudly for him to understand what you were saying. This I think resulted from the many years of his skeet shooting days so he often had to wear hearing aids throughout most of his later days. With the wind blowing and Herb's irritation with the whole project he was in no mood to be told what to do about anything. He had a very brusk manner about him at times and was quick to temper despite his benevolence generally.

Somehow in the next few minutes as Herb was fighting the wheel I looked over my shoulder and to my great horror and great embarrassment were two gentleman farmers, probably the land owners of the farm just staring down at us with their arms crossed. I was mortified to say the least as I knew we were indeed caught with our

Herb Weichert and his girls

"pants down" in this very uncomfortable situation. In an increasingly loud manner essentially repeating his name over and over, Herb discounted my attempts to communicate and continued pulling and prying on that crazy wheel. He didn't have a clue what was happening and the two farmers just stood patiently staring down and I of course I was feeling the brunt of the embarrassment and shortly thereafter Herb must have noticed their presence and things came to an abrupt halt. I don't remember what was said but I'm sure I mumbled with great apology as to what we were up to and probably tried to make an excuse that we thought we were still on the Kott Farm. I am sure they where quick to tell us that we were in fact not, but for whatever reason, God knows, they acquiesced to our taking of their property and turned and walked away. I don't remember if I offered to pay or whatever but I still found it very strange that these fellows were being so generous.

In any event, that wheel came back with us all the way to Alaska and I subsequently mounted two birds on it and it came out quite nicely. It is currently in the possession of Herb's son, Herb Jr. in Valdez. At Herb's going away way party for his retirement we had made a large poster illustrating him bending over that wheel and me gesturing to him the frantic situation that we were in. It certainly got a lot of laughs and was even mentioned at Herb's memorial service that we had in Valdez. Cindy still laughs about this and I'm not sure where that big poster ended up but it sure captured the moment.

That is the story of "caught with our pants down" and one I flash back periodically as a head to the Dakotas each year. I still maintain contact with the Kott family and I would try my best to bring down fresh or smoked fish each time I would stop by their home. I hope to see them one time again time but energy will dictate if that happens.

The Innoko River Fiasco

Sometime during the late 1980s, Paul Barret and myself came up with the plan to float the Innoko River, which is part of the famous Iditarod dog trail and is accessed from the small village of McGrath that is on the Kuskokwim River. I had researched this from one of the local taxidermists that had taken a number of giant moose off of the Innoko River however he had the benefit of aircraft, which we did not. Our plan was to float a relatively long section of the river from an abandoned town called Iditarod down to what is known as Cripple Landing, which is located at the halfway point of the Iditarod dog race. This section of river is noted for having a multitude of sand bars and ideal for having moose feeding along the area that would be accessible and visible from a raft or boat. Paul was a long time friend of mine who began his law practice in Valdez and then moved on to Fairbanks where he became a very successful and prominent partner in a law firm. He spent most of his off-times doing extensive river trips throughout the interior of Alaska and was very knowledgeable on traversing the rivers which requires a fair amount of understanding of the currents and avoiding perilous situations. We had maintained contact over the years and I always regarded Paul as one of the brightest persons that I ever knew however one has to deal with his stubborn single-mindedness which is part of his character, unfortunately he tends to be right most of the time.

As previously noted, I had gotten a fair amount of information from one of the more famous taxidermists, a fellow named Brent Jones who still is in the business of bear hunting on the Alaska Peninsula. Brent had pretty much done everything in the state and gave me great details of what to expect on this particular float trip. The plan was to take my 14-foot inflatable boat with a 15-horse outboard and transport it to McGrath where we would then take an air taxi to our starting point. This in itself was quite a task as the boat and motor and all the additional gear probably amounted to well over several hundred pounds. Nothing remained in the little town of Iditarod except for a few buildings. There was some type of a landing strip that put

Captain of the Innoko

us relatively close to the river. As we discovered from the landing strip to the river itself was a monumental task as carrying an outboard that weighed probably 60-pounds, gas and the raft which is probably another 100-pounds that length was quite a feat in itself. The real spectacle that I remember the most was the craziness that involved the local air taxi. Alaskan bush taxis are notorious for poor maintenance and often times irresponsible with less than experienced pilots. The young pilot that was going to fly us to our destination seemed to be a native fellow who looked not much older than 17 or 18-years of age. We found ourselves in an array of aircrafts, most of them in ill repair which left us with a bit of uneasiness for sure. The first plane we tried was a Cessna, probably a 185 and it failed to start so we unloaded onto another aircraft and this one had a flat tire so we proceeded to try our next airplane that was again, fully loaded with our gear and as we made our way down the runway the door actually came off of the airplane so our young pilot just parked it and we were onto the fourth aircraft. This was a tricycle wheeled airplane not designed for landing on bush-type airstrips. I vividly remember trying to land on this gravel strip near Iditarod and the speed in which he approached the strip was way beyond what I was comfortable with. It was clear that this plane was not designed for this type of landing situation and we were relieved that he was able to safely slow it down and bring it to a safe stop. So this began the craziness of an almost nightmarish trip, the details of which I hope I can capture. Needless to say we never did see that pilot again although the plan was that he would make provisions to pick us up at Cripple Landing approximately a week later.

We began the float rather expectantly with the great anticipation that we were going to find ourselves bumping into multiple large moose but soon discovered that the water conditions were high and the weather deteriorated. The first overnight camping was on a sandbar that was almost completely submerged by the next morning as the river rose and the rain increased in veracity. As the days rolled on the rains were unceasing and our trip soon turned into a very uncomfortable survival venture. All of the sandbars that we were expecting to find on our way down were already under water, which made access to seeing moose very unlikely. Putting up a tent in the rain is no fun and then of course taking it down the following morning makes it even more uncomfortable as all the gear tends to get wet and damp as you're unable to dry things off adequately. The good news was that my little Evinrude motor saved us from having some disastrous outcome because of the sweepers that seemed to be increasing in numbers namely large trees and brush that would be hanging into the water which could result in getting hung up and getting sideways, potentially upsetting the raft. The motor was able to safely navigate around these dangerous sweepers. Fortunately the raft was a very stable one and again with Paul's expertise in navigating the river he did most of the motoring and we were able to make our way down the river at an increasing rate, not what we had expected of course. Some days later we found ourselves at what we deemed as our destination as the cabin of Cripple

Landing was visible from the river and we soon discovered that another raft with all the provisions including a moose were stranded in a nearby island type of area and it was apparent that the owners had left the equipment there as they were unable to navigate the raft to the landing strip and again the water levels were rising exponentially. The sandbar that was to be the landing place for our return aircraft was under several feet of water and we knew we were in for a long wait. As we made our way to the cabin which at one point was a lodge of some sort and had been there for seemingly many years was already occupied by four other individuals. They too had found themselves in a predicament and had been sitting there for a number of days already waiting for conditions to improve so some aircraft could pick them up and return them to McGrath. We were able to venture out to the area where the raft and moose were situated and I'm sure the fellows that owned it were very thankful that we had arrived and able to salvage their gear and trophy. They offered to split the moose meat with us but at the point we were not particularly interested in this additional burden.

The lodge at Cripple Landing was a very interesting abode that had a long history of visitors and as previously mentioned it was the halfway point of the Iditarod and was occupied by the mushers many of which would stay there and rest before proceeding. The walls of the lodge were absolutely filled with every imaginable piece of memorabilia and pictures, and you could spend hours looking at all of the interesting items and trivia. In the back room of the lodge were cases of wine and champagne that were obviously used for celebratory activities when the teams would have made the halfway point. I believe that the winning musher got somewhere in the neighborhood of $5,000 in gold coin if they were the first team to arrive. In any event we were scratching our heads as to what to do and the only thing was to grin and bear it as best that we could and each day that passed we would go down and check our marking sticks to see if the water level was lowering and I remember it wasn't going down at a very fast rate. We did not have any means of communicating with McGrath and this certainly would have been a situation where a satellite phone would have been invaluable. On future trips I often carried a satellite phone for this very purpose. As it turned out one of the group that was there had some previous communication arrangements with his wife and he assured us that somehow his wife would be making some phone calls if she had not heard from him. One of the interesting dynamics that occurred at the lodge was that we found out that the two groups, both father and son couples had made this trip before and at one point

Solitude - Paul Barnett

were the best of friends. However, at some point they had a major falling out and had not spoken with each other for some time and now they found themselves stuck together in this uncomfortable situation. The tension however was not that obvious and we didn't find out the full extent of the animosities until after the fact. As noted, each day we would go down and check the water levels which did not seem to recede very quickly and it was apparent that the sandbar landing was not going to be a reality and that it would take an amphibious plane on pontoons to get us out of there. It seemed that on day three or four of our stay at Cripple Landing a floatplane emerged and landed on the river. It turned out to be one of the more noted air services and guides, a fellow named Magneson who was very well known in the McGrath area and owned a lot of operations in that locale. It seems that like many of the villages in Alaska there are always one or two entrepreneurs that dominate the businesses whether in home rentals, stores or air services and the Magneson's were one of the more prominent families for sure. The first person to be bailed out of the predicament was the more adamant individual who had again had made arrangements for his wife to call in case he wasn't heard from. He left with his son and we later found out that he left the bill to be paid by his adversary and this eventually turned into a civil court matter. The air service obviously new our predicament and charged well over $1,000 for our return trip to McGrath and they obviously took advantage of the situation. When we finally got into McGrath the errant person had already bailed out of McGrath and had jumped into a commercial airplane and was already on their way to Anchorage. Subsequent to this trip, Paul was deposed for the purposes of providing a witness to the arrangement that we understood was going to occur, namely we were going to share the expenses of the air service bill. I do not know what the outcome of that court proceeding was but it was a strange twist to this story. Paul vividly remembers all of the particulars of this God awful trip that we got into and blames me for talking him into it in the first place. One little interesting side note was that Paul maintained his Jack Daniels whiskey sipping as we floated down the river and I on the other hand was only drinking Kool-aid. This later came to haunt me as a I got a severe case of giardia while Paul obviously had purified his drink with whiskey and killed all the parasites. I paid the price for not filtering out that water and it was clear that it was probably not suitable for drinking as it was very murky and we saw indeed an abundance of beavers as we proceeded and as one knows giardia is often referred to as "beaver fever". Untreated it can result in some very serious consequences, namely the parasites can get into your internals and liver, etc. and can involve some rather extensive medical treatment.

One notable thing in all of the memorabilia that we saw in the lodge was a picture of the famous actor Charlton Heston and it appeared to have been taken sometime during the 1940s when he was doing some type of hunting in those days as a young man.

The air service that originally dropped us off never even bothered to even contact us and I can't remember whether we had paid them for the initial service or not but they obviously had little concern about our well-being nor took the courtesy to find out whether we were safely picked up or not. Again, this is not an unusual commentary as air services in Alaska are notoriously disorganized and you have to be very careful in picking and choosing the service you're going to be using however often you do not have the luxury of having more than one service available in any particular area. To my knowledge they never made any efforts to talk to another air service for the pickup although that might have occurred without our knowledge.

I did have two other trips to McGrath, again a notable jumping off place for hunting as the area is known for its large moose and the wild herd of buffalo that are in the Farewell Burn Area approximately 75-miles from McGrath. The buffalo trip I took with George Maykowskyj, who at that time was the superintendent of schools, is worth re-telling and one I might go into some detail on later. The other involved a trip with one of the local celebrities named "Lucky Egress" a half-native fellow who was one of the more notable pilots in the area who specialized in wolf control and turned out to be a very competent woodsman as he had was born and raised in McGrath. Aerial hunting of wolves had always been a controversial subject in Alaska and at times has been allowed but then the anti-hunting groups would intervene and get it shut down. The moose population in McGrath has been reduced dramatically because of the predation of wolves and bears and in my trip with Lucky we found ourselves traveling well over 100-miles down river to find moose availability. This in itself is a very expensive chore for the locals as gas prices are well over seven or eight dollars a gallon and the cost of securing their subsistence meat for the year is greatly effected by this expense.

Lucky

I had an occasion to make a trip with Lucky Egress. He had originally contacted me as he got my name from good friend, George Maykowskyj and Lucky was looking for a shooter when he was doing wolf control with his Super Cub. However, as it turned out the aerial shooting was precluded because of outside regulation but I did manage to work out an arrangement for a potential moose trip with him. I had made an arrangement with him to pay all of his expenses, namely the gas that it would take to get us into some good moose country, I think somewhere around 1995 I somehow found myself back in the village of McGrath. Lucky was part native Alaskan and I think his father was a good ol' Norwegian. From the onset I could tell that Lucky was a pretty competent guy and knew his way around the country and obviously had spent his life exploring and learning how to live this subsistence lifestyle.

One little anecdote that occurred prior to our leaving was that I found myself in one of the two local pubs in McGrath and I had picked the wrong one. As I was sitting at the bar the bartender was obviously intoxicated and he confronted me accusing him of something to do with money that I had on the bar. I later found out that this was the bar that the out-of-state or out of town white man does not go into as it is exclusively a native bar. Soon I found myself surrounded by several other native fellows that were there to intervene and as things were getting a little out of hand, in strolled Lucky his presence calmed things down and his only words were "we are going to leave now". I would guess he was highly respected and probably feared by most of the local native folks. Lucky was a pretty strapping young fellow and I'm guessing at the time in his mid to late thirties.

The plan turned out to be a trip down the Kuskokwim River and he was a little vague as to what the destination was but his brother had been down to an area where they had soon a lot of moose and he was heading in that direction. One interesting side not was that he did not fill up his boat tanks until the morning of our departure, as it was never a good idea given the thievery that goes on in the village. In the native culture the communal rules somehow dictate that everybody shares the bounty and there are no bounds on what is yours and what is mine. It was clear that Lucky was not going to be party to losing a hundred gallons of very expensive fuel.

The next few days found us whisking along on his jet powered outboard and the miles seemed to go on forever. The colors were changing so there was certainly a beauty in the air and in the surroundings. After what seemed like 8-10 hours of speeding along we found ourselves in the evening and coming up upon another group that had setup camp for the night. It was all part of the tradition of moose hunting that had gone on, I'm sure, for millenniums in the area so I was party to the evening festivities which was sitting around the fire and listening to their stories and chatter.

The next day found us again going down river for what seemed like another 4-5 hours until we came to a small tributary that went off and at the juncture was a small cabin that obviously had been there for years. That became our abode for several nights and it was welcomed as there was rain in the forecast. The following morning we made our way slowly up this relatively small river area and the magic of Lucky's knowledge and skill became abundantly clear. He used the shoulder bone of a moose as we stopped at various points he would rub it on the trees and I swear that each time we stopped he was able to pull in a bull moose, something that I found truly amazing. It was right in the mid-term of the rutting season, I think it was either the second or third week in September and as the bull moose come in they will often emit a low grunting noise and swing their antlers from side to side and this is called "displaying" as they are trying to show their dominance to what they think is another bull in their area. The first bull that came in was so close that we had to essentially shoe him away as he was well within archery range if I had brought along my equipment. We kept holding out for a larger bull but during the interim, Lucky made a an astounding shot at a smaller bull and without a word being said he went flying off the front of the boat onto the shoreline and it looked to me that he had intentionally wounded the moose and was now running it down to an area that he could access the animal more readily. I heard a shot go off and sure enough what had happened is that he dropped that moose on a bank right next to the river where he could easily load it onto the boat. It was quite a remarkable feat if that's what he intended and suspect that was the case. Watching him dismember that moose was quite a spectacle because he only used a knife and

was able to cut through the rib areas and certain joints that most white men would not even know how to do. He would cut hand-holds in certain parts of the quarters so they could be slid into the boat and he made it look so easy that it was humbling to watch him. One embarrassing episode during this process was my efforts to help and as I grabbed a quarter of moose and slide it off the bank into the boat it came sliding down at a rate not expected and hit my legs, knocking me half way out of the boat with my head dangling in the water. Next thing I knew I felt a strong hand grabbing me and pulling me out of the water and I'm sure he just shook his head. I was good and wet so that's what I got for my helping efforts. Shortly thereafter it seemed again as if magic was in the air, Lucky called another bull moose in that was in the trophy class, probably close to 60-inches in width but unfortunately it was not close to the river and this created another situation that he was not happy with. The moose went down but extricating it was another story in itself. I had hoped for a larger trophy sized animal but was pretty much told that he had to get his son who was in our company back to school so all of the moose was loaded into the boat and we found ourselves once again pounding the river as we made our way back to McGrath. It seemed to me that we made the return trip at a much faster rate so we must have been going downstream with the current and that made quite a difference in our return time. The moose horns were eventually shipped from McGrath to my home in Soldotna, Alaska at the time and they hung on my garage doors for a number of years and then either given or donated away to one of the neighbors. I was very impressed with Lucky's competence and I see where he had acquired the name so appropriately. Interestingly I heard that not that many years ago that he was dating our neighbor lady in Valdez but I don't think I've ever spoken with him since but do have flashes of my trip to the Kuskokwim River.

60"

Chronicling a Montana Goose Hunt Live

Over the past fifteen or twenty years I have made my way to the Yellowstone River just east of Billings, MT, approximately 80 miles in the small town of Hysham and it seemed to be the hub of all of the migrating geese. Often it was in the latter part of November that the geese would show up as they would find their way down from Canada and down from the Dakotas as their water would be freezing. The Yellowstone River for the most part would stay open in this section and was surrounded by miles and miles of fields that provided good feed. I had the good fortune of meeting a lady who owned a small bit of property east of Hysham named Shirley Warren. Shirley was a very hospitable older woman who had spent most of her life as I understood on this piece of property and she generously allowed us to hunt on the pasture area that was adjoining the Yellowstone River. This particular spot was great as there was a bend in the river and there was a large island adjacent to the shore that provided a natural haven for geese. I was always worried that Shirley was going to lease the property which often occurs and money people from Billings or surrounding communities would offer farmers major dollars to have exclusive rights to the property but Shirley in her tenacious way said there was no way she was going to lease her property as she was going to pass it on to her kids and grandkids. A few years ago Shirley passed away and her daughter, Hanna has also been most generous in continuing her mother's legacy. I've always had great luck hunting this bit of property and would set up a blind off of the river and basically wait and watch as the birds would move from the water to the fields and there was always action to enjoy. Over the many years I have brought a number of friends there and we have en-joyed this little piece of property immensely. In 2018 I had the brainstorm to drag a recorder down to my blind and thought it would be interesting to capture the nuances of the day as they developed. Each venture always brought a different venue of happenings and frustrations as the case might be. Some days would go smooth with great shots being made and birds cooperating. Other days they were so spooky that they would fly too high and not show any interest in this particular field and the few decoys that I would have spread out before me. However, on this particular day I thought I would try to chronicle the day and the various little special moments that would make it unique. So one early morning I brought my two trusty dogs. One being my old girl Sara, age 13 and Fergie my new dog, just barely one year. Containing the dogs in this little blind was always an issue and I had both of them tied down so they would not over react and spook any incoming birds. This is particularly true with Fergie who is very intense and this was a new experience for her and I knew I was in for a busy day with her. My little blind was basically on the base of the high water mark of the bank and I had it camouflaged to a fair degree. On that particular morning there were several hundred geese within 100-yards of the blind and in the darkness I was able to sit in my blind and not disturb them. As I sat there I could hear the increasing cacophony of noises as the geese became increasingly excited as the morning light rose. The old term of "noisy goose" is certainly understandable as one sits there and takes in all the raucous noises that they make and depending on the weather conditions their level of honking increases I think they somehow encourage themselves to make the first flight of the morning. I have found in cold weather conditions that they often won't leave the water until late in the morning and sometimes as late as noon. However this particular day was moderate weather conditions and I knew they would be leaving the water soon. Often the case is that they have been smart enough to avoid flying close to the bank area particularly if there's any brush and they will often get up and circle high and go down the center of the river usually with a predestined location to feed for the day. Often in the morning it is not very productive as I mentioned as the group seems to have other places on their minds and they will seldom if ever look at my small spread of decoys. However, once in awhile I will have some singles or doubles show some interest and that would be the opportunity of the morning. These large western Greater Canadians have very organized patterns and they will revisit the same field if left undisturbed, often leaving in the morning and returning late in the morning to rest up and then they will go out again in the afternoon for another session of foraging. In this way they are more predictable than for example snow geese that seem to be very erratic in their patterns. The lack of water in this area with the exception of the river has actually been has been a plus and I have noticed that the birds will return sometimes several times during the day to water and then return to the fields and this has been very helpful as I

John Tongen - Montana Limit

find that sometimes the action is most intense in the late morning and early afternoon times when they are coming and going. On this particular morning I found myself in the same scenario and it's quite a spectacle to listen to the noise that's almost constant and keeps one on alert. It's often those that are not honking that will sneak up and you'll find them over your decoys before you're able to react. As I spoke into the recorder I was trying to capture the moment and I think some of the noises were probably actually being recorded as the geese were very close that particular day. It seems that as the morning gets lighter the noise level increase as if they are trying to encourage themselves to make the big move for the morning flight. With that, the dogs seemed to also become more agitated and in tune with what was transpiring. Fergie seems to be even more reactive and her agitation level and tail wagging is markedly more evident. My old girl Sara has been through the routine enough that she sits more quietly and seems to know the drill. She still however has the instincts and I often watch the tail wagging on both of them to get a feel for their interest and intent. There was a time when I used to use a coffin blind which is a layout blind that you lay flat down and I remember having both dogs, one on each side in their with me and as the birds would be coming, the wagging of the tails was so intense that they were beating on my legs with increasing velocity. It also was a source of great warmth and comfort although it is difficult to stay in that layout blind for an extended length of time as the comfort level is not there and also it takes a great deal of practice to shoot from a prone position.

As I was recording the day's happenings I was constantly looking from side to side not knowing in which direction the geese might make their appearance. As if orchestrated, as one flock makes to the air it kicks off a succession of adjoining and neighboring birds and all of a sudden the air is full of birds going in all directions. That particular day I remember things were happening in a very successful pattern, which is often not the case. I had multiple opportunities of birds making their way close enough to my blind that I had more birds on the ground within a couple hours than I ever expected. Every day is different and one doesn't know what to expect which makes it all the more exciting. Certainly one's shooting prowess varies from day to day and one miss will often lead to a succession of misses and this pattern could continue for the whole day. On the other hand when one seems to be in tune with the firearm, there is an automatic instinctive reaction that seems to carry you through the day with great success. I should note that for whatever it's worth that I have been using, for a number of years and throughout most of my life, a side by side double barrel shot gun and I have currently been using an L.C. Smith vintage shotgun dated 1928 and because of it's age one has to use special shot called Bismuth which is quite spendy but indeed very effective, certainly more effective than the steel that is now required in all states. In the old days lead was the preferred shot but because of the issues regarding lead poisoning of waterways, etc. the Federal government passed a regulation precluding its use. In any event, my old L.C. Smith has been a wonderful piece of history and I often do extremely well when I am on point.

I have done goose hunting off and on most of my life,

however I never really successfully got into it until I moved to Montana, although I did do some hunting in Prince William Sound and also in the Delta Junction Area in the interior of Alaska. My poor old father always wanted to get a goose in his career but never succeeded. It seems in our youth the geese were not as prevalent and often they would migrate through our area without stopping. Now their pattern has completely changed and they have become in some cases a scourge for some cities as they have found refuge in areas that they never were before. They actually have discovered that to stay put and not migrate to the south is a safer route and may also be indicative of the global warming issue.

As I was sitting that morning, my little dog Fergie was becoming increasingly agitated and jumping around and before long I was having to deal more vigorously with slowing her up and quieting her down. As the geese are approaching they are very tuned in to any movement or anything that looks out of place and a jumping dog is certainly something that would catch their attention and they would quickly react. During the first recording of this tape I was able to capture some of the noise levels of the geese that were very close. It was soon after my arrival in the blind that the first goose came tumbling down and Fergie went ballistic trying to break loose from her tether, pulling the blind partially down and causing me a great bit of distress as I tried to unleash her and let her retrieve the bird. She is extraordinarily fast and was soon all over the bird but has not quite figured out how to physically pick it up because of its size and Sara on the other hand has mastered the technique and knows to grab the bird by the neck and pull it along. Fergie on the other hand will jump all over the bird and often tries to pull it by the wing, etc. and this is something I'm still working on with her. The particular day that I was doing this recording was the day in which I was shooting extraordinarily well and couldn't seem to miss. This is often not the case. I have found that getting the first bird or two down will often set the stage for one's shooting prowess for the remainder of the day. The trick with geese in particular is that they appear so large that they don't seem to be moving at the rate of speed that they actually are and one will not often give them sufficient lead and thus the bird is missed or unfortunately wounded. If one can swing enough lead and hit them in the head or neck area they come down stone dead whereas hit in the body area, their thick down feathers often will preclude any mortal injury. One has to continually talk to themselves about concentrating on the head area and then leading accordingly. Try as I may I continue to make the same mistakes although some days certainly go better than others.

There is some extraordinarily effective ammunition these days but the cost is so expensive that it's hard to justify its use. On the other hand, wounding birds is not in my comfort zone, for sure and I have observed other hunters in fields wounding multiple birds, as they will often have some delayed reaction and sail far away and not be retrievable.

On that particular morning, as noted, the day was alive with birds and there was seldom a time when I could not hear or see birds in the air. Canadian geese are very smart birds. Their eyesight and their instincts to avoid humanity are often amazing. I have been told by a seasoned guide that he has noticed that Canadian geese will often sit and let the lesser geese, i.e.: snow geese, white fronted, etc. leave first and will listen to where the shots are coming from and then go in the opposite direction to safer grounds. They have become increasingly adaptable as I have mentioned and in many places in the country they have become a nuisance, particularly on golf courses where they enjoy the easy pickings but are the scourge of the golfers that must walk through all of their mess. Snow geese on the other hand, continue to make their extraordinary migrations each year and their numbers have increased appreciably to the point where they have opened liberal seasons not seen since the 1930s. Spring hunting is now allowed, the use of electronic calling devices and limits that are extraordinary have done everything to try to decrease the numbers of these birds. The biologists have determined that in some of their breeding areas and nesting areas they have done significant damage to the point where their future could be permanently destroyed and it is hard to believe that kind of damage could happen given the vastness of the northern Canadian Territories.

As that morning progressed, most of the birds flew up in a great roar as I had expected and ended up flying high above the banks of the river and heading in various directions. I think the only single bird I got was a loner that found his way close to the decoys. So as I sat through the morning I was looking forward to the return of birds between 12:00 and 2:00 in the afternoon. I think this is a strange phenomena in this area but the birds seems to act completely different when they return from the fields, often coming back in small bunches making themselves more vulnerable as they will take a look at my decoys and if luck is with me they will come within range. I have upgraded my decoys over the years as the geese have become increasingly more adept at identifying decoys from the real thing. Some of the newer decoys are what they regard as flocked and have a texture that makes them look

Limit on the Yellowstone

lifelike. The natural feather patterns are captured in the molds that the decoys are made from whereas in the old days, decoys were carved out of wood. The other change has been showing change in the movement and the newer decoys are on a pivot device that reacts to wind. Up in the far north, I think some of the natives of the area still make decoys from mounds of dirt and will do some flagging, basically movement to pull the birds into their direction. However, as the birds progress down their migratory route they become increasingly smarter and can soon identify a decoy spread. So I have found that earlier in the fall the birds are much more vulnerable for decoying than those that have shown up later in the fall and have probably been shot at more than a few times.

In my youth my dad was always very nostalgic about the geese in the fall and would always remark about their 'V-like' formations as they made their way south. It was always indicative of another winter coming and the passing of fall was captured in a piece that he did before his death in 1980. My father was able to read into nature's patterns as part of one's life cycle and I think became a bit melancholy as the years passed.

That particular morning that I was doing this recording was a bountiful one and I had five or six birds down in relatively short order as the day progressed. The greater Canadian geese average between 9-13 pounds and even five birds creates quite a load to deal with. As this little story progressed I noticed that I was using the various times of the day and morning to make my notations. I remember one of the highlights was of a bird falling from a great distance that was not expected and hit the ground a bit lively and my little Fergie took off like a speedster and hit that bird like a linebacker. Then of course, she didn't know what to do with it but held on to it Sara finally caught up with the situation and her masterful way just picked the bird up and as if to show the new girl what to do, she dutifully brought it back to the blind. I think on that particular trip a number of birds hit the river and I think both dogs were successful in retrieving them although there was probably at least one occasion that the bird hit so far out that the bird got into the current and was not retrievable. One little scenario that occurred that day was almost a subtitle of a poor old goose that wouldn't die. I believe either Sara or Fergie had dragged it into the blind area and I had thrown it in the bushes only to look back within the next few minutes and the bird was gone. As I perused the area, low and behold that crazy goose was almost down to the water's edge where it would have disappeared for sure. Sara with her bad legs was quick to react and made her way down the bank and grabbed that bird and dragged it back close enough where I could retrieve it. After dispatching the bird I once again threw it in the bushes and not many minutes later I looked up and that goose was once again finding its way down to the river and poor old Sara once again charged as best she could and saved the day. I deemed that goose the one that wouldn't die and it added a bit of chaos to the morning and I didn't need the exercise as I had to make my way down a rather slippery slope that led to the rocky beach that was often also slippery. While springer spaniels are not noted for being waterfowl dogs I have over the years to have had springer's that were great retrievers and as it turned out, both

Sara and some of my other dogs have been extraordinary swimmers. Fergie is probably the strongest swimmer that I had and early on she made her way three quarters of the way across the river and I found her well over one half mile down river where she finally caught up with that bird and got it to shore. I am again blessed with a new friend that I think will be a great performer if I can keep up with her. On that particular day I think we achieved our limit by one in the afternoon and I was exhausted by all of the happenings of the morning. As a note, I have found goose meat to be palatable and I have discovered that the breasts can be made into some wonderful salami, which is done commercially. The legs on the other hand, I will boil and make a wonderful soup that I enjoy and have shared with others that have concurred. The next day of that particular trip was also a banner day, however I was finding myself increasingly more worn out by the end of the day. One of the issues with sitting in a blind is that you're constantly twisting and turning and it wears out old bones and joints so I've finally arrived at getting a small swivel chair that I situate so that I can swing from side to side as necessary and it does save on the back and bones. One other little happening that day that I recorded was as I looked out onto the river I could see what I determined to be the belly of a goose floating down the river. My new little dog with some hand signals automatically picked up on my direction and found herself mid-river and retrieved that goose. It was obviously one that had been hit earlier on and was in good shape so Fergie at only a year old was becoming a natural already. I'm sure there are more than a few geese that will make it to the river and finally die of their inflictions throughout the night and I would guess that was the case with this particular bird. I should note that the river is constantly being cruised by golden eagles and I think that they pick up many a cripple if not all as they fly the area and scavenge birds that have not been recoverable. As I remember this was the first occasion where I saw the dogs getting competitive over a bird. This can often occur with strange dogs and the instinct of a bird dog becomes obvious when another dog will approach what they have deemed as their bird. I think I noted that Fergie and Sara got into a momentary scuffle over a bird that had already been claimed by one or the other. That second day I succeeded in getting the tenth bird which was my limit for the two days and we left with a very strong sense of having a wonderful outing with both dogs performing well and my shooting also better than usual.

The Year of the Wolf

Over the many years that I've found myself in Valdez, I've always wanted to catch myself a wolf. The wolf is notoriously known for being so wary that those have been successful in catching them are usually those with great experience and expertise on the wily ways of the wolf. Valdez with its great snowfall seldom allowed for a wolf to be in the area although occasionally there is one seen here and there. The one phenomenon of note was a small number of moose that seemed to have thrived in the area and their only survival mechanism was to move out into the river flats area during the height of winter where the snow levels would be considerable lower. Otherwise they would not be able to fight their way through the voluminous amount of snow that blankets the area. I used to try in vain many a time to catch a wolf and following my retirement I in fact succeeded in catching one up in the 60-Mile Country probably by pure accident had sought some advice from a serious wolf trapper who lived up in the Tok area. In fact I spent several days with this young gentleman and he was a madman of energy and used to catch well over twenty wolves a year but it was a 7-day a week struggle and of course he had the availability of a snow machine and his father had a Super Cub airplane that allowed them to find moose kills that would be idyllic for snaring incoming wolves. I did pick up some tips from him and finally did succeed in catching a wolf in a rather strange occurrence. I had put a lynx cubby set and had seen some old wolf tracks so I encircled the area with snares in hopes that a passing wolf would find himself entangled. It seems that it was in the 2009 in mid February when the weather took a dramatic change and it created a unique situation. I believe the temperature had dropped to as low as 45 degrees below zero and in those conditions I did not risk the dangers of trying to go up into the pass area and then down into the creek bottoms. Remarkably the weather did a complete change-about the following week later and temperatures rose above freezing and there was almost 100-degree temperature differential, which was extraordinary. With that I headed back to where I had made this particular set and was looking about and concluded that something looked rather strange and sure enough, one of the snares that I had placed on the trail was gone and I found myself circling and there to my amazement under some light snow was a deceased wolf who was in a very contorted position. My elation gave way to the prospects of having to drag that wolf up a rather steep hillside along with my gear and on snowshoes. I remember that my adrenaline was so high at that point that I succeeded in ultimately hurting myself. The best I could do was to pull a few feet as I got into the steep areas and tie off the snare on a tree then move up a few more yards and pull and tug and then re-tie and this is how I manage to achieve this minor miracle. In my younger days I probably could have done it with little effort but this was not the case at this point in time. Unfortunately this ordeal of pulling, tugging and twisting of my back created a resurgence of an existing back condition that changed my life. I succumbed to surgery later on that year and the botched circumstances created some ongoing nerve issues in my right extremities that I'm still suffering from to this day. So my pursuits of the wolf cost me dearly. The surgical calamities that followed still remain a sore point in my memory but best not to perseverate on the details.

In 2011, for whatever reason, and I suspect it was a

One of two wolves - 2011
Very few in my career

combination of an increasing local moose herd and snow conditions that were not severe so we found ourselves inundated by a large pack of wolves that had never been seen to my knowledge in the valley. Some of the local boys, including James and Ricky Wade and Doug Cranor all the young fellas that I had know for some time were telling me that they had been spotting moose kills in the valley that they had never seen before. They were quick to take advantage of the situation and had borrowed snares from me and were successful in catching several wolves in short succession. The ability to spot a moose kill and to find a fresh trail into it creates an ideal situation for snaring as it allows one to predictably put the snares in the best locations along these routes. The number in the pack was in question but they were guessing there were at least twelve to fifteen and as things developed they were seemingly killing a moose almost every few days. With this in mind I began in earnest to look at some familiar areas where I had previously seen wolf tracks in years prior. One area in particular was along a salmon stream where both bears

and wolves would often find themselves wandering as there was a late run of silver salmon that would stay there well into the winter. So with that in mind, I put a number of snares along the creek bottom in specific spots that I thought would be productive and to my delight I found a wolf in one of my snares following a substantial snowfall that I think must have camouflaged the snare and the critter was caught by his hind leg and was quickly dispatched.

This elation however, turned to a desperate situation as I discovered probably within several hundred yards of the snared wolf, was a young bull moose with a snare around his nose. I often tried to put snares in the area where moose would not travel or put cross-pieces over the snare to preclude them from going through a particular spot but there I was with a very lively moose. The snare was around his muzzle, which made it even more precarious, and he had a good bit of distance to move as he was fighting the entrapment. My first inclination was what to do and my mind turned to the Wade clan and James in particular who I thought if anyone could figure out how to extricate the situation, that he would. James is one of the more adept individuals that I have met in terms of outdoor finesse and I have embellished some stories of James in other chapters. On that particular day I made my way to their home and with a bolt cutter in hand we headed back to our predicament. James and his cat-like manner, being very quick of foot and is certainly much more stealthy and athletic than I, approached the moose in a very slow, methodical manner to see how it would react and sure enough its first instinct was to charge him and I can still see James quickly moving to the side as if he was a matador avoiding the horns of the bull. He made several more attempts to get close enough to snip the snare wire but each time he was met with a charging bull that he so casually avoided. Finally for whatever it was worth, he was able to get close enough to snip the wire and fortunately it did not get all of the threading which was a godsend as it still contained the moose allowing us to back out of the situation and with a few swings of his head, the snare gave loose and we were able to see him make his retreat. I thought for sure that the pure exhaustion of being snared would have led to his demise just out of shock but I was relieved to see that the following day he was still moving about and was able to shake loose the noose that had been around his muzzle but the crease was still evident but hopefully he survived the winter.

Some weeks after that I had put a large leg hold trap in the creek itself where I had noticed other wolf crossings and behold I found a very pretty light colored wolf sitting there one afternoon when I arrived. So two wolves in one year was indeed a banner one that I never repeated. The larger of the wolves I mounted life-size and it came out quite nicely and was displayed in my shop for some time. I believe I subsequently donated it with some regret.

Before the winter of 2011 had ended I'm guessing that the pack numbers had been reduced at least by half and this would certainly allow for the remaining moose herd to have a better chance at surviving the remainder of the winter season. The debate over wolf predation is ongoing but the bottom line is that they do considerable damage to herd animals like moose and caribou and here in Wyoming, particularly in Yellowstone Park, some elk herds have been reduced as much as fifty percent. Often times but not always, wolves will kill for the pleasure of killing and I know on one occasion that both Ricky and James spent hours trailing a wolf that was pursuing a cow and the damage done to that poor animals as they tore chunks from its haunches in an attempt to bring it down. At some point the wolves gave up the chase but the cow was found not far away having died from exhaustion and shock. James, in his expertise with the snow machine and his pure prowess, could tell many a wolf story and later that winter he had found where a pair of alpha male and female wolves had killed another moose near the Richardson Highway and had torn out the fetus and left the scene.

James managed to follow those wolves to the pinnacles of a nearby mountain and was able to catch up with them and that in itself was a story that I would like James to share. So that ends the story of the year of the wolf and one that I will never see repeated. In my communication with some of the fellows in Valdez there has been no sightings in recent times so the wolves obviously have retreated back to the interior where they can more comfortably manage the snow levels as they look for prey. The wolf will remain one of the more idiomatic critters of Alaska. One is struck with how wily and tenacious they are and on the other hand can also see that left without control they can do terrible damage to the environment that they share with man.

The Wade Clan and the Mountain Goat

One afternoon in late December James Wade came by the house and told me that he had been sitting with his scope and had noticed on the far mountain behind our house was a mountain goat that he viewed as being seriously injured. The birds were circling and he could tell that something was amiss and he had noticed this same goat in the area for the past three days. So the day after Christmas we decided to go up and see what the situation was and whether in fact the goat should be put out of its misery. I made my way with the two Wade boys, Ricky and James who I managed to keep up with although we had to snowshoe probably a thousand feet vertically after we got to the base of the mountain on snow machines. I found myself ascending with some relative ease even though I was up in age and keeping up with those young legs was usually not an easy task. As we got to the hump, which was actually a large rock, we were surprised that the goat did not seem to be in the area. So we ended up circling down from that peak and sure enough James in his usual acute manner picked up movement even though everything was a haze of white and you could see that they poor goat was struggling to get back up the hill to his little rock sanctuary. After the goat was put down it was obvious that it had been seriously injured, the bullet having gone through an ear and into the hump area, which was already infected with gangrene. The entire hump area and shoulder was a green mass and that animal would have had a miserable death, as I'm sure it had not been eating and would have eventually died. The other part of the hide however, was in relatively good shape although after mounting it I had to replace a section in the shoulder as well as the ear but the end product was quite stunning as long winter hair and face was certainly striking. The long beard coupled with some sizeable horns was estimated to be probably a goat of eight or nine years of age. Goats generally do not survive beyond the age of twelve or thirteen.

As long as I'm talking about goat hunts I would reflect back on one of the original hunts that I made in the late seventies on Allison Lake, a lake that sits above the Aleyeska

Terminal at about twenty-five hundred or three thousand foot level above the tree line. This was prior to the '9-11" fiasco and I'm sure that accessing the lake above the terminal would have gotten us into some security issues in later years, however, in this instance I talked to my friend Walter McGehee to try our luck and I had already been given a tip by another fellow that he had been observing a very large billy goat sitting on the glacier above the lake and he assumed that it was not in good shape and so with that information we proceeded to make arrangements to be dropped off at the lake. The lake itself is idyllic and this particular day it was crystal clear and the fact that we were above the tree line made things far easier. We landed at the far end of the lake and then the next day we started trekking up the glacier and could already observe that the goat was up in that area and had moved up into more steep terrain so we determined to go around and get above the critter and have a better vantage point. The view from our point was extraordinary as we could look down and see Valdez across the Valdez Arm and all the way into Mineral Creek which is the valley that goes north out of town and is a perspective that one seldom has the occasion to view. That old goat turned out to be a very large animal. The body size was huge and his horns were broomed from its age that was estimated to be at least thirteen years. He

Christmas Eve

had absolutely no teeth left in his head so God knows how he was making it through the days and it was probably highly unlikely that he would have survived the winter. Walter actually spotted another single goat farther up on the glacier and again we pursued that one it unfortunately turned out to be a nanny. It was unusual to find a single nanny as they are usually with larger herds.

The real irony of this story developed later in the trip as we waited patiently for the return of our air taxi. This gentleman was a local fellow that had only been in town for a few years but had started up his air service and was busy transporting hunters and fisherman around the Prince

William Sound. The pickup day was to be in the afternoon, however it was apparent that things were going to be questionable as the weather was deteriorating badly and the cloud level was dropping and we knew if it dropped much further that the visibility would preclude him landing on this little lake. However, on or about five in the afternoon the airplane made its way into the lake and we were comfortably transported to a lake that we were very familiar with outside of Valdez. I remember him mentioning that he had one or two more pickups that day at Silver Lake, which is also a mountain lake that was above Galena Bay approximately fifteen miles down from our vantage point.

The Final Product

The weather, I assumed, had probably deteriorated even further by the time he made his arrival and disaster struck in a very terrible way. Apparently he came into the lake at too fast of a rate and the lake itself was like a mill pond and I know float plane pilots always are concerned about their ability to ascertain their distance to the water as it gives a false perception. Apparently when he hit the water at a speed that was not appropriate he somersaulted the aircraft, which ended up upside down. The pilot and the passenger struggled out of the aircraft and were sitting on the pontoons while the hunters he was to pick up watched as they frantically tried to paddle the craft to shore. Meanwhile, I was told that the hunters were trying to construct a type of raft to get to them but had to watch in horror I'm sure as the plane sunk and the pilot and passenger went down with the aircraft. It came to mind that we could have had an equal situation as this occurred only an hour after he had made our pickup and had for some reason, I had even taken a picture of the aircraft that evening that I still have. Silver Lake is extraordinarily deep and the plane and passengers were never recovered.

The Rock Pile Elk

In September of 2004 I had an opportunity to take a relatively cheap bow hunt near Lewistown, MT. It was on the famous Lewis Ranch that had been there for one hundred years or more and they allowed only a few hunters each year and they were exclusively bow hunters as this ranch manages thousands of angus cattle and I'm sure they did not want rifle hunters shooting about. In any event, this was an idyllic hunt for me because it was the last hunt of the year in the fourth week of September and he had only three other hunters aboard and working with small groups is more my cup of tea as opposed to some of these large lodge type hunts that get more chaotic than I care to deal with.

Two of the gentlemen on this hunt were what one would called a gung-ho bunch and gave all the appearance of being ex-Marines in their manner and dress. They were young, energetic and very aggressive in all that they did. I laughed quietly to myself as I watched their rituals, which were done in synchronization, be it dressing at the same time and they would go through a calisthenics procedure each morning and evening and would put on their night lights at the same time and appeared to have been bunk mates at some point, maybe during the military. They were however, very much to themselves and didn't really give me much information nor did I intrude on their privacy. I understood that they had been at this camp one other time so they were absolutely adamant that this was going to be the trip. Interestingly they had used my guide person the previous trip and had opted to go with the chief guide who in fact had the lease with the ranch. I could see that they were going to approach this hunt with great gusto and I swear they had at least three pairs of boots and every manner of gear that could be expected like they had just walked out of a Cabela's catalog. Every morning they were up and about and they were bound and determined to cover that ranch in any manner possible and I got the impression that they were covering miles and miles each day coming back exhausted and empty handed as it turned out. For me, I had decided that I was going to take a different route and my guide whose name eludes me at this point brought me up into some high mountain fields that had obvious elk signs everywhere. The first evening I sat in a very high tree stand that was extremely uncomfortable and didn't feel particularly safe to me. Later that evening a cow elk came out but I was so uncomfortable that I couldn't have pulled that bow back if I wanted to. It was my decision to create a ground blind in a corner of this field and stick it out in hopes that other elk would make their appearance as the evening approached. The elk usually hang back in the heavy timber then show up late in the evening and spend most of the night feeding and return to protective cover in early morning. I found an ideal blow-down of a large tree and created a pocket that I could comfortable sit in that gave me access to the corner of the field and that's where I spent at least three days. It seems that on the third day that my guide friend who was only there to get me situated left a silhouette cow decoy on the edge of the fence line approximately forty yards from my little ground blind. Later in that morning it was raining hard and this is indeed unusual for Montana, as it seldom seems to rain in that part of the country. So hunkered down in my abode and sat there patiently with water running down my face and I for whatever reason, glanced to my left and to my astonishment was a large bull elk making his way down the fence line and I could still see the water running off of his muzzle as he approached. If I had my wits about me I would have got my bow into shooting position but was a bit dumbfounded as the bull got closer he was broadside and it would have been the perfect opening, however, in a split second he was obviously surprise by the decoy and made a large bound directly into my space. I swear within ten or fifteen feet away and I was eyeball to eyeball with this large shaken critter. I could have easily speared him but as it was the archery equipment that was fumbling in my hand, the arrow fell off of the rest and the bull made one final leap and over the fence staring back at me quizzically as I sat there shaking my head in disbelief. It was a golden opportunity lost and an experience that I will probably never repeat. As I remember, the bull was certainly of trophy quality. He was a six point elk, which is what everybody pursues and I will probably never have a chance like that again. As I sat in the blind most of the day I noted that in the evening I could hear bugling and activity that was farther down the field from where I had been sitting. I could not see what was happening but I knew that elk were making their way into the field at the other corner so it was with some consternation that I decided that maybe my best bet would be to relocate and see what was actually showing up in the

Pope & Young Book - Montana 2004

evening at the opposite end of the field. As I perused the area, there were a number of spots that I could situate myself but I decided on a large rock pile relatively close to the edge of the field. I thought that I would sit there behind that rock pile and be in the position to see what was coming through the area. Sure enough as the evening grew dark I could hear a bugle in the distance and to my amazement I saw a line of elk coming my way parallel to where I was sitting I think at least seven or eight cow elk strung out and one by one they made their way by my rock pile about forty-five to fifty yards away. I knew that at the end of that long line of cows might be a bull and sure enough one appeared and I almost instinctively without much preparation let an arrow fly and could see that by the reaction of the elk that it had hit true although I did not know exactly where the arrow had struck. The action of the animal showed that it had been mortally hit and it stood there and again, this is very unusual as most animals hit by an arrow usually take off at a dead run and finding them always becomes a feat in itself. However this elk just stood there somewhat shaken and I knew that something seriously was wrong as the cows came by and rather sadly looked for him to follow, which he did not. He made his way very slowly and I knew that he indeed had some serious injury. By then the evening had given way to darkness and I tried to follow up where I thought he had disappeared to but had no luck in finding any evidence nor did I find the arrow. Curiously, my two bunk buddies happened to be coming by the area and mentioned to them that I just had a shot but they were in a rush and didn't seem to have much interest in providing me help.

Later that night we returned with large headlamps and searched the area with no avail. My two buddies I remember even as I was sitting at the cabin pondering the fate of the elk and had no questions to even ask and I think were disgusted that an old man like myself would have been potentially successful and they had nothing to say to me which I thought a bit strange and not very kindly for sure. The next morning found us back in the area and sure enough the elk had only made its way less than one hundred yards into a thicket with the arrow protruding from the liver area which is why it reacted the way it did. If anyone has ever watched a prize fight and have seen the boxer hit in the liver area they will notice that the legs go out and essentially all of the air is expelled and they are pretty helpless and this is obviously the phenomenon that I had observed. The elk was a nice one but certainly not of trophy quality however, it was a six point and did make the minimums of the Pope and Young record book for whatever that is worth. As we returned to the camp area my two buddies never even asked nor showed any interest in my success and wouldn't even look into the back of the truck where the elk laid out. I guess they found some dark humor in the whole situation.

The unfortunate follow up to this story is that we brought that entire critter to a butcher shop that dealt with game animal processing and they hung it up put it in the cooler. I think the total weight was somewhere in the neighborhood of seven hundred pounds with the head off and field dressed. Several weeks later I got a disturbing phone call that the meat was bad and he referred to it as bone rot. Apparently the fact that it laid out all night created heat that penetrated from the bone and contaminated the meat. In my Alaskan days we often in almost all cases would bone the meat on the spot and I guess we should have done this that morning and I'm sure would have saved all of that wonderful meat that was lost. I think the amount was somewhere in the four hundred pound range as elk is highly coveted in the west. So ends my story of the rock pile elk.

I could reiterate another little scenario that occurred during this hunt as it was one I still remember with great detail. One morning we could hear the bugling of an elk and it was obviously moving into the dark timber and we stealthily moved along listening for the calls as they occurred and we found ourselves getting closer and closer to the noise. If you have not heard the bugle of an elk, certainly it remains one of the thrills of nature. As we closed the gap sure enough this extraordinarily large bull elk was probably fifty to sixty yard ahead of us and he was magnificent in all ways. His antlers were extremely large and I could see the shiny white tines in the morning sun. As I begin to draw my bow back somehow he inherently picked up our presence and turned from broad side to moving straight away moving slowly but yet there was not a shot available. It remains however a sight that I felt worthy of mention that many people never have an opportunity to see an animal of that magnitude. It was a great stalk and we did everything right but close the deal as they say.

The Cabin on Shearwater Bay, Kodiak Island

In the mid 1980's the state of Alaska offered one of a number of opportunities to put in for what they referred to as "remote parcels". This was indeed a grand opportunity for those that wanted to secure some land in remote places in the state and it was on a lottery system as more ideal places closer to road access, etc. were highly coveted and the drawing odds reflected that. This particular parcel was available on one of the bays of the south side Kodiak Island approximately fifty miles west and south of Kodiak City itself. However, to get to it, it requires a relatively long boat ride or the use of an aircraft. I was fortunate as it turned out to have been successful in the lottery and the next task was to stake the acreage that I believe the maximum that one could stake was five acres. I looked at a number of areas and the one that I felt would be the most successful was one on the very far end of what they call Shearwater Bay, which is part of a much larger bay called Kulida Bay. A good friend of mine and one I have mentioned before, Rick Richter who offered to take us down there in his 185 Aircraft. Also accompanying me was my good friend George Maykowskyj, as I have mentioned before is a jack of all trades and had some experience surveying, which proved to be invaluable. He even had access to some survey equipment that came in more than handy. This particular parcel was maybe ten or twelve different pieces although the predicament was that it was located approximately five hundred feet above the water level on a plateau type of area and it did involve making a big hike up a hill and when we arrived that evening there were already several people awaiting the time frame to begin which I believe was the following morning at eight a.m.. Everyone scrambled up the hill that morning and we found ourselves picking the far lot that abutted up against public lands and George and his skill with the survey tools was able to scope out our five acres and we dutifully put in the stakes at the four corners and had completed the first of a task that turned into a monumental one in later days. Even the survey process was rigorous as this property was a spongy tundra like mixed with at times thick alder patches that had be to cut in order to string a survey line down the areas that we were trying to encompass.

So ended the beginning of a process that took over five years to achieve given the bureaucracy of the State of Alaska and the paperwork and all of the requirements that were dutifully required. The major issue involved having it officially surveyed by a licensed surveyor and I spent a good bit of time trying to find someone willing to take on this task, one being a gentleman in the Kodiak that had access to a airplane and or helicopter but told me that the expense of a helicopter would be sizeable. It seems that it took several years of cajoling before in fact he finally succeeded in getting down there and officially surveying the property and putting in all of the necessary metal posts that are required by the State of Alaska. Then came the paper chase of submitting the survey and waiting for the State of Alaska to approve the application. This seemed to take forever, and I know I made multiple phone calls and inquiries before I got the final paperwork approved and before long, I had a fair investment involved. I think the survey itself was somewhere in the five thousand dollar range and the State of Alaska had its computed appraisal of the property at another five to seven thousand dollars although they did factor in some discounts of which I can-

Cabin Site - George M. doing his magic

not remember the details of. So approximately five years after we originally staked the property we had a full legal paperwork to authenticate the ownership of this piece of Alaska. During those five years we made several trips over that way deer hunting and were quite successful however we had to tent it and one particular tenting venture turned out to be during a brutal December snowfall that we paid dearly for the few deer the we did manage to get. Somewhere in the 1985 timeframe I found for sale what they called an igloo, which was essentially a metal conical hut that was used in extreme remote locations as it could be dismantled piece by piece and transported to areas where it might be necessary. It truly looked like an igloo because it was white and because of its round shape it was able to withstand the winds and rigors of remote artic places. I can't even remember where I bought that from and I can't even recall the expense although I think it was in the neighborhood of three thousand dollars and I recall it had an approximate 12 x 12 floorplan and it came in pieces, essentially it was a pie shaped sections that would slide into grooves and be bolted together at the top and by a ring on the bottom. The weight itself was somewhere around five hundred pounds. So began the great building escapade and once again I had the good fortune of having the expertise and willingness of George Maykowskyj to pull off this building expedition. Transporting that material with additional plywood, etc. originally went by Sea Land transport shipped to Kodiak where it was stored until we could make arrangements until we decided how we were going to get it down to the building site so the expenses mounted given what we had to deal with and I trudged ahead with stubbornness in hopes that I could have a remote cabin site that would be useable for whatever purpose but it was a dream just to say that one had a piece of Alaska that you could call your own. Transporting those materials to this site was a chore in itself. It required chartering several aircrafts one being what was regarded

as a Goose, which was regarded as a large amphibious aircraft that had been around for many years and the other
was a I think a 206 Cessna that could take the remaining
pieces and parts and our gear. It was quite a chore just to
fit these pieces through the narrow doors of the aircraft
but somehow we managed to do it and on our way we
found ourselves flying to the site. As things would have
it, we unfortunately miscalculated the pathway we had
chosen to make our way up the hill and the aircraft landed
short of this spot, which created a whole other issue that,
we found ourselves in as we unloaded and discovered that
we were well beyond where we should have been. As we
piled the materials on the beach we shook our heads with
disbelief at how we were possibly going to move this pile
of wood and metal, the first chore was to get it to the base
of the hill, which was at least five hundred yards away.
This in itself took well over a day of handling each piece
and dragging it through the rugged pathway that led to a
very steep incline. Fortunately, we were energetic and had
some strength of body and mind to undertake such a an
ordeal. George, as I remember, captured some or most of
this on video which I have someplace and George's frustration with this whole project was evident in his commentary as we struggled to put this together. It remains
probably one of the more crazy things that I undertook

The dome put together by George Maykowkyj

and again I was more than grateful for George's willingness to take this one. The next two days were extraordinarily excruciating to say the least. The hill that we had to drag each of the pieces up was not easy and we did it step by step and went from one plateau to another and then made our little campsite next to the materials and would start again the following morning. We had brought along a small one-wheeled device that we tried to use to facilitate the moving of material up the rather narrow pathway that was strewn with alders and was always slippery and difficult to manage. Later as we returned, I again found myself bewildered at how we ever managed to get that amount of material up that hill. I know by the time we arrived at the summit of where the site was located it was indeed a herculean accomplishment.

We originally thought we could make some kind of base work that would act as pilings for the foundation but soon discovered that digging them in this ground was not going to work. We ended up laying cross pieces of four by fours as a makeshift foundation that they cabin would sit upon. By then, time was ticking by and the weather was not improving and we knew we had limited time to complete this task before the aircraft would return. The critical portion of this whole project was that each of these pie-like pieces of metal had metal louvers on each end that had to perfectly slide up to couple and any damage to those louvers would have made the task impossible. Fortunately, somehow throughout all of the transport and man-handling of this material it did in fact all fit together, again thanks to the ingenious and perseverance of George who could always figure out how to make things work. Needless to say there were many moments of frustration and invectives screamed into the sky as we struggled with the task at hand. God knows what damage we did to our bodies in the physicality involved in man-handling all of this weight but I'm sure we have had all paid the price for the things we did in those days.

That little cabin still stands today and I have been back to it several times over the years although, I did recently sell it to a real estate fellow who went to the property once and I don't know what he plans to do but I think his age precludes its use. As we found out, getting up to it with gear was very problematic and it remains the only structure on this entire parcel area as the other people that had interest obviously did not pursue it, maybe for the obvious reasons.

We did do some upgrades to that cabin in the following years including some lighting, insulation and some heating. We made at least a couple hunting ventures and the most memorable one being a bear hunt where I actually did get a permit for the area and took a friend namely, Chris Moore who was a young and energetic fellow who made everything look easy because of his youth and vigor. He was a mad man of energy and hunting and adventures were his sole interest in life. I had kept a diary in that little cabin for a number of years and Chris went into some length of our bear venture, which turned out to be a fiasco given the weather, which was unrelenting rain for eight days. Chris unfortunately died in an airplane accident several years after our bear hunt and the notes that had written in this diary are no longer there and I can't believe why someone would have taken that diary. I know over the years that the cabin probably had some use from people that would see it on the hillside but it remains one of the crazier things that I did in my younger days. One little side note that I wanted to mention was that as a manager of the Harborview Mental Health Facility in Valdez late in the nineties we admitted a gentleman called Wild Bill Winecoop. Bill, as it turned out was a fascinating character whose dementia had reached such levels that his obstreperous ways had found him excluded from every nursing home in the state and he found his way down to our facility that specialized in managing behavior. As it turned out, Bill had lived in a cabin literally ten miles from where our cabin was and he had been in a small bay area on the far valley called Eagle Harbor. Bill had been there for fifty years and had commercially fished and was a noted character in every regard. As his health deteriorated and his state of mind became such that he was institutionalized in Kodiak but was forcibly removed because they could not deal with his cantankerous ways and combative behavior. However, with my time with Bill at Harborview we talked about his many experiences on Eagle Harbor and he was very familiar with Shearwater Bay as he would sometimes walk the entire valley trapping and knew well the area. He was a bit of a mysterious gentlemen and the State of Alaska was always trying to find the funds that he had apparently hidden someplace as a result of him selling his commercial fishing boats but they were never successful in finding his bank roll, if in fact he still had one. One interesting note was that I don't think Bill ever had a family and he told me somewhat secretly that at age 16 he had been party to a bank robbery in Seattle and that is why he escaped to Alaska and lived in the bush as he had done. Whether this is a true story or not, this was something that he conveyed to me shortly prior to his death. His remains were scattered back over in his home area of Eagle Harbor and this was done by a friend of his who also had some special connections with Bill. So ends the story of the Shearwater Bay cabin and I thought it well to reiterate some of the struggles and crazy dreams that were pursued in those younger days.

The Wade Clan

I have made mention of some of the experiences that I have had with the Wade family. The Wade boys made their way to my home at approximately age 18 where they sought some taxidermy help with a shed antler that they had found. They are the grandsons of Milford Taylor and Bonnie Taylor and the sons of Becky and Rick Wade Sr.. The Wades had always been an amazing group including the older sister, Rhonda, as they seemed to have some astounding skills in areas, from making dives to recover sunken boats to all manner of handling major equipment. They have an uncanny sense of how to figure things out and are by far some of the more resourceful people that I have had the pleasure of knowing. I know Ricky in his earlier years used to make dives to check for leaks under

the huge tankers that arrived in Valdez. A very precarious job to say the least to go into that cold arctic water and go down fifty to eighty feet. I know they were still finding ways to raise various boats that would be sunk and the knack and know how was always amazing to me. Rhonda also would chip in on all occasions and could handle equipment as good as than the boys in some cases. She was an accomplished photographer and taught self defense courses in taekwondo. Ricky developed his own trucking business and still finds time to explore the vast mountains and dales with all manner of equipment, most recently the acquisition of an aircraft that will indeed lead to a new dimension. I also appreciate the fact that both he and his brother have maintained contact with me and still let me know about some of the adventures that they have found themselves in so in some respects I'm still living vicariously the Alaskan dream.

Rick and Becky's youngest son, James, I have always had a special admiration for as I have found him to have some innate qualities that I can truthfully say I have found in hardly another person with the exception of John McCune. James truly is in tune with the wilderness that he finds himself in, often by himself but he has the ability and almost inherent sense of how to get himself out of the most difficult situations. He is probably one of the most competent four-wheeler and snow machiners in the Valley and is often crowned "The Kind of the Hill" every year during the hill climb competitions. He himself could categorize a multitude of experiences that he has had, often capturing them on video, some extraordinary with regards to wolves, bears, moose and sheep. He tracked a very large moose for a number of years and I had the occasion to see that magnificent critter and I do have a picture of it. I'm sure I've never seen an animal that large. James could certainly put on quite an exposition of his own with some of the video pieces that he has taken and still has the youth and vigor to make many more experiences and trips. His patience always inspiring as he can sit behind a spotting scope for hours on end and can always manage to find some elusive critter that he is looking for. He also is in the process of purchasing an aircraft and this will certainly expand his horizons and I look forward to seeing some of the adventures that I know he will be creating in the future. James is one of the few people that I would trust my life with and even more as recently as last summer of 2018 we took a one hundred and eighty mile round trip in a small jet boat unit in some very precarious conditions and he somehow magically is able to find his way up some of the most difficult tributaries and always finds a way to do it safely and with such ease and confidence. So I wish

Jame Wade 60" Moose

good luck to both of the Wade boys who have always been so good to me.

As recently as last year, James sent me some extraordinary pictures that are hard to imagine. He took these pictures over a number of days and it was in video form and was quite stunning. He found two bull moose fighting to the death, which is unusual in itself, and one was finally critically and mortally injured and laid there for several days before its demise. In this instance the smaller bull, somehow because of his horn configuration he was able to literally mortally injure the larger bull, which was a gory sight in which James explained he could hear the painful cries of the larger moose as he was being gored. James captured all of this on video and later found an even larger bull moose that was also dead and he assumed it was the result of his confrontation with this feisty smaller bull that cut into the vitals of the larger animal with his antlers. All of this is extremely unusual as typically the dominant bulls will usually have a brief antler banging episode and then the less dominant one will retreat but to have a smaller moose actually kill a larger bull moose in the same area is indeed unusual. In any event, James captured this episode and it seems like this is something that he should have put into some production. He also captured on video a brown bear while waiting for the demise of the injured bull moose and the bear waiting patiently for several days for the animal to die and the film footage was most interesting. James had later taken that bear with a friend. Bear predation in the area has long been an issue as they will kill almost all of the young calves in the springtime. There is a very liberal season on bears in that area for that purpose. This is but one example of some of the things that James seems to find himself in the midst of and he often will send copies of his video to me that I find enthralling.

The Kamchatka Peninsula Experience

Somewhere in the year of 2000 I decided that I wanted to venture over to the far east of Russia namely the Kamchatka Peninsula that is not all that far away from the Alaskan mainland. At that time it was easily accessed as for the first time the Russians were allowing tours into that part of the country. Previous to that it was a highly secured area because of its submarine base and air force. Both Alaska Airlines and Reeves Aleutian Airways made ventures over there and one could find themselves in this extraordinary country within five or six hours flight time from Anchorage. As one approaches Kamchatka you can still see the fighter aircraft in camouflage dug out and it is truly a step back in time as one wanders the local city that is in very poor repair. It is obvious that the economy of

Russia is indeed in dire straits as there is little activity at the airport, I think for the lack of fuel and other resources. They have however, seen the value of the American dollar through tourism and the unexplored Kamchatka Peninsula that is known for its abundance of brown bear and some extraordinarily large moose and several varieties of sheep. Unfortunately, some of the early years there was an excess of exploitation and unethical means, such as shooting from an aircraft, was allowed to the detriment of the population. I had an occasion to make two ventures to the Kamchatka Peninsula and both of them were indeed interesting in one way or another. I still have hopes of making a return to Kamchatka but now the access requires a round trip through Moscow and the air time is daunting.

My first venture was probably the most memorable as everything was new and very exciting in many ways to find yourself face to face with a completely different culture and itself was an experience worth relishing. I remember quite vividly how our first trip over there as we crossed the Bering Sea which is an exceptional piece of white vastness that we somehow ended up landing on a small island that I really didn't identify. I assumed it was to refuel in case, for whatever reason, the weather would not allow us to land and we would have been forced to return to Anchorage. Approaching Kamchatka is indeed like going back in time. It feels like somewhere in the 1940s or 1950s and you could tell that there has been very poor maintenance of the town and that life is very simple and the economy poor. I have not tracked it in recent times but it was apparent then that things were barely functional and the infrastructure was poorly maintained and I know from some communication with the locals that life is truly very austere. I don't know how much of this was a reflection of the breakdown in the Russian Federation that occurred in the 1980's but I think the entire Russian country has been in dire shape for some time. Dreary would be a word to describe what one feels driving around the city viewing the local environment. On the other hand, the local people still seem to take pride in their appearance. The women walk rather stately and the men are usually adorned with their sable hats and while people do not seem particularly friendly, we did find that when we were in a different environments, particularly in the camp areas, we found a more warm response from the people we were dealing with. This was not necessarily the case with some of the guides as most of them were ex-military and I do not think that they particularly like Americans and still harbor bad feelings towards the U.S.A.. However one is struck with a certain sadness in the eyes of many of the people and I did have this explained to me by one of the interpreters that said this was a reflection of many years of poor living and strife which probably began at the onset of World War II where the Russians suffered extraordinary losses I'm guessing somewhere in the nine million range. The people had to survive the best that they could and that melancholy still seem to prevail in their countenances. The people that live in the Kamchatka Peninsula are a bit of a cross section of many folks, probably similar to Alaska. It is a melting ground for people that come from the west and my interpreter, for example, was a young gal who worked in an office in Moscow. However, many of them I think did work for the government particularly the military and I think with the changes in the economy the living wage was often elusive. One interesting note was that our pastor from Valdez, namely Father Mike Shields, decided in his mid-thirties to divest himself of all of this belongings and try to restore some measure of Christianity in the city of Magadan, the end of the Trans-Siberian railroad and was also the site of the infamous gulags which were essentially concentration camps that were setup during the Stalin regime. Multiple thousands if not millions of people were transported to this remote location and many failed to survive as they were put in unbelievably brutal conditions. They still refer to those that experienced that as the "survivors" much like the holocaust people of Israel.

Father Mike was instrumental in having a church built and has been an inspiration to restoring Christianity, which had otherwise been done underground during the Communist rule that prohibited any public demonstration of faith. We still maintain contact with Father Mike and as recent as last year he made an appearance in Valdez as he would periodically travel to Alaska and other states to secure donations for his ministry. He is an amazing individual and when he is in a room one is certainly aware of his presence; charismatic would best describe him.

My first go around in Siberia was indeed an interesting and fun one as the group I was with were from a variety of areas from New Jersey to Texas and Montana. They all had interesting life stories and were quite a group to travel with. We traveled via large military-style helicopters that one would wonder how well maintained they were. They were loaded to the gills with God knows how much equipment and provisions and getting off the ground at times was quite a feat as they tended to literally bounce them up and down trying to gain enough air speed to make an ascent. Given the price of fuel they tried to maximize their trips into the local villages and I know we were bringing a lot of provisions that were being dropped off in some of the local areas. On our first venture across the peninsula to the west side we found ourselves in the midst of a severe blizzard and the conditions worsened to the point that visibility was almost nonexistent. At some point the pilots made a dramatic decision to put the craft down outside of a small village. It was indeed one of the most humble places that I have ever seen, very similar to some of the villages in Alaska. We found ourselves begging ourselves into a fellow's small house where we all slept on the floor that night. Despite the crowded conditions he was most hospitable and I believe everyone left a generous donation for this magnanimous willingness to put us up for the night.

The leader of the group was an interesting gentleman who sticks out in my mind. He had a certain charismatic presence about him and his name was Victor Emerits, former military colonel. You could tell by his dominant personality that he was used to giving orders and he did so quite vigorously. Everything seems to revolve around his decision-making and this included occasional sit-downs where he would organize a picnic type of affair where salami, cheese, etc. was distributed and he would basically be "holding court" so to speak and did so with a rather gregarious and jovial manner. It was obvious that he was fully in command of all that was occurring and that all business conducted was done with his approval only. Needless to say, vodka was present at every gathering and the Russians are notorious for their drinking patterns, which represents one of their few luxuries. It takes very little occasion to get into a vodka toast where tiny little vessels are passed around and there is a lot of celebratory activity that occurs often and for no good reason.

On this first venture we found ourselves dropped off at a remote camp where there were tents that were set-up on top of a hard snow pack. They were comfortable to an extent but certainly not any luxury for sure. The cook tent was separate as was the God awful outhouse, which was some distance from the camp and hard to deal with. Each day started early and it was often cold and we be on the back of sleds that were being pulled by rather archaic looking snow machines. We would left while the snow conditions were hard and we would go looking for tracks of migrating bears that were moving from their denning area to the ocean where they would scavenge for food. Finding a fresh track and then pursuing the critter was the order of the day, however in this instance we were not very successful in finding fresh signs. I had interestingly talked to two gentlemen who had been in this exact same place two years before and had seen over fifty bears and had taken some very large ones but on this trip that was not the case and it was truly slim pickings. I ended up al-most mistakenly taking a relatively but absolutely beautiful blonde bear and was less than pleased but it occurred in the flurry of a moment in thick cover were we really didn't properly judge the quality or size of the animal. As it turned out there were a few other options and there was only one bear of any size taken in this trip. However, overall it was still a memorable experience and one of the highlights being immersed in the culture and we passed Easter there where they went through some of the traditional rituals including the cracking of eggs and a number of other local customs that was of great interest. When we arrived back in the Petropavlovsk I also had the opportunity to get into the middle of their May Day celebration, which is the highlight of the year and is symbolic of the end of World War II and the Russian victory over the Germans. All of the televisions that were available were all strictly controlled by the government and were all documentaries of the Russian conquest and the end of a brutal war that decimated a good portion of Russia, particularly places like Stalingrad where I think three million people essentially starved to death during the German occupation.

The one thing of note regarding the Siberian bear that I found extraordinary is the hair quality. I was told by someone later that the Siberian bear does not have the mite that often causes the Alaskan bears to scratch during hibernation and result in a rubbed hide. The bears that

Pretty good bear

I saw were exceptionally furred and luxurious. The Russian fur is known as the best in the world particularly the Russian sable and everyone seems to be wearing them. In downtown Petropavlovsk there were marketplaces where one could buy furs but we later found that importing them into the States was another story and I remember in some cases a number of hunters losing fur products and particularly bear claws that have been embellished and all were confiscated by the customs personnel.

A year or two later I decided to make another venture back to Petropavlovsk through another booking agent who turned out to be a bit of a scoundrel. This trip, however

Old Military Chopper

went more successfully in some ways as I did manage to get a bear during the last days that was acceptable in size and was mounted life-sized and recently sold to someone in Australia I am told. This trip I had made explicit plans to go in earlier than most and stay later in hopes of improving my opportunities to find a truly large bear. This required days of harrowing snow machining over extremely rough conditions including the crossing of homemade bridges any of which could have resulted in some serious injury. I was always amazed at the resourcefulness of the Russians and they would literally tear the machines apart each night and redo the parts as needed, thus the fact that all of them had the same equipment and were able then to exchange parts. The modern snow machine would be of little use to them as any break down would not allow them to be repaired. The electronic ignitions that are prevalent in all of the new snow machines would be a real detriment giving the unavailability of parts. These machines looked ancient but were very dependable with one front ski which allowed them to make sharp turns and bends and move through the wooded areas in a very easy fashion whereas the standard two ski snow machines would have a much more difficult time traversing some of the terrain that we found ourselves in. Again, I always remarked on how resourceful they were in keeping those machines together. At one time during a blizzard the ski actually broke off and somehow my guide went through his toolbox and figured out a way of putting that back together and we made our way safely back to camp.

The small base cabin that we found ourselves in was remarkably uncomfortable and the number of people that ended up their was problematic. Somehow through a miscommunication a group of fellows from Denmark showed up there and that further exasperated the crowded conditions. I found myself sleeping in an out-building that was used for diesel storage and found the nights almost impossible as the odor of diesel almost made me nauseated at times. However, the group was a jovial one and there was a lot of interesting commentary made despite the fact that English was not necessarily the dominant language that was spoken. The interpreter was a lovely gal whose mother lived in Petropavlovsk and she would come out to the camps and would make more money during her weeks out in the bush doing interpreting and she was very articulate in a number of languages. Most of the hunters left early with mediocre bears but I stayed in the camp for a couple more days and I was able to find a bear that was at least an acceptable size in the eight to eight and a half foot range. It was mounted life-size and was in my taxidermy shop for a number of years and always drew positive comments. I don't regret my trips to Russia and often think that I would like try one more trip but this is pending some decision making as of this writing.

Ironically Harry

A fellow named Harry Chapin remains one of my favorite musical artists of all times although his music dates back to the 1960's and 1970's. Some of his music ended up being quite popular although he was more known for his concerts and various appearances around the country. Unfortunately, I was never able to see him although I did at one point have an opportunity in Seattle but missed it. What struck me with Harry was his story telling and his music was intertwined with a message and a tale that unfolded as he sang. I don't know how much of it was a reflection of his own personal life but I would suspect some of it was. The irony that occurred was that I had a number of things that kept bumping into me as life unfolded beginning as early as the seventies when a friend of mine gave me one of his records and or CDs at the time. In Alaska, particularly in the earlier years there was very little music available and the radio stations were very local if any and one had to depend on your CD or whatever mechanism that could be used in the vehicle. Harry somehow struck a cord with me and I started listening to his stuff from early and continue to do so until this day. The funny connections that I seemed to have run into bare telling and someone might find some amusement and coincidence in it all.

*Not Harry but George and big goat -
Cold Christmas Even*

The first situation occurred in Massachusetts where the Chapin family can be traced back to its very origins and apparently some of his family were the founding fathers of Springfield, Massachusetts. My son just so happened to be living in Massachusetts and low and behold he ended up buying a Queen Ann style home built in the 1850s on Chapin Street of all places. During one of our visits I found it most curious that his young son going to bed each night listening to some of Harry's methodical songs and that was all a bit coincidental for sure. For those that are not familiar with Harry Chapin he was an interesting a brilliant fellow. He was I think, well-educated and came from a family that was very service oriented and Harry took up a number of causes during his brief lifetime particularly that related to poverty both in the States and around the world. He was instrumental in founding one of the world hunger organizations and devoted most of his concerts to generating funds for that purpose. I know he was a political activist and testified in congress on several occasions and I suspect he was an anti-Vietnam War advocate. What made his music so interesting was the tangled web of storytelling that occurred with each of them and I found it very soothing but also applied it somewhat introspectively. The one song of particular note is titled "Cat's in the Cradle" and I could relate to some of the story line as he essentially I think felt guilty because he was gone from the family so much and wasn't able to devote time to his children and in later life when he was looking for attention from his kids they of course had moved on and had their own lives so it was a bit of life unfolding and I in fact thought it was worth attaching here:

Cat's in the Cradle by Harry Chapin

My child arrived just the other day
He came to the world in the usual way
But there were planes to catch, and bills to pay
He learned to walk while I was away
And he was talking 'fore I knew it, and as he grew
He'd say "I'm gonna be like you, dad"
"You know I'm gonna be like you"

And the cat's in the cradle and the silver spoon
Little boy blue and the man in the moon
"When you coming home, dad?" "I don't know when"
But we'll get together then
You know we'll have a good time then

My son turned ten just the other day
He said, thanks for the ball, dad, come on let's play
Can you teach me to throw, I said, not today
I got a lot to do, he said, that's okay
And he walked away, but his smile never dimmed
It said, I'm gonna be like him, yeah
You know I'm gonna be like him

And the cat's in the cradle and the silver spoon
Little boy blue and the man in the moon
"When you coming home, dad?" "I don't know when"
But we'll get together then
You know we'll have a good time then

Well, he came from college just the other day
So much like a man I just had to say
Son, I'm proud of you, can you sit for a while?
He shook his head, and he said with a smile
What I'd really like, dad, is to borrow the car keys
See you later, can I have them please?

And the cat's in the cradle and the silver spoon
Little boy blue and the man in the moon
"When you coming home, son?" "I don't know when"
But we'll get together then, dad
You know we'll have a good time then

I've long since retired and my son's moved away
I called him up just the other day
I said, I'd like to see you if you don't mind
He said, I'd love to, dad, if I could find the time
You see, my new job's a hassle, and the kids have the flu
But it's sure nice talking to you, dad

It's been sure nice talking to you

And as I hung up the phone, it occurred to me
He'd grown up just like me
My boy was just like me
And the cat's in the cradle and the silver spoon
Little boy blue and the man in the moon
"When you coming home, son?" "I don't know when"
But we'll get together then, dad
We're gonna have a good time then

It seems like I always had Harry on the radio as I made my way around the Alaskan countryside, particularly those days when I was traveling back and forth from my trapping expeditions and it became even more poignant as I discovered that his music was being played out on the east coast as my son's home. Across the street from their home was a large cemetery and in one corner there was a large array of Chapin headstones across quite a number of years and I assumed that Harry was related to those Chapins in some fashion. His family was quite well-educated and his grandfather was a noted artist and his father and other members of the family were writers which contributed I'm sure to the fact that Harry seemed to be very intellectually keen and had a philosophy on life that you seldom here from today's artists. Not more than three or four years ago or so we were in the Springfield area and at the local theater a concert was being put on which was essentially a musical portrayal of Harry's music. Each done with actors and a specific storyline that went with it. I was able to get an even better understanding of some of his lyrical lines and we attended the concert on a Saturday evening. Interestingly, we missed meeting his widow who had just been there moments before and had been in town for the express purpose of seeing the theater performance. I would have loved to have said hello to her and maybe could have relayed some of my attachments to her husband and his music. Approximately two or three years ago the family did a book on the life of Harry and his family published by his wife and one of his sons. I purchased that book and was astounded to see some interesting correlations again including the fact that he was born in the same month and year, only a few days from my birthday on November 19th. There was an interesting picture from when the family had taken a trip to Alaska. I swear the picture looked like the Valdez glacier, which was more evident during those early years, and I would have loved to asked whether they had been in Valdez because that is where we were at the time. Harry's life ended in a very dramatic way in 1980 when he was on a rush to a concert and was involved in an accident that took his life. It would have been interesting if Harry had lived a longer life as I think he was able to generate music that has significance and would have provided some depth of meaning you often can't find in today's music. From what I could gather, Harry was always in a mad rush to move from concert to concert and I suspect the day he died indicative of his passion to be someplace and perform. I've noted this with several people in my time that almost have an inherent sense of their lives being cut short and the are often the ones that seem to be so much in a rush and I think they know subconsciously that they have to cram as much life into their given time. One other individual, namely Chris Moore, who I worked with his wife for a number of years. Chris was a fellow I hunted with on more than one occasion and had a mania about him where he had planned every hunting venture for a year ahead of time and was always in a mad rush to get someplace and do something. I often wondered if Chris somehow subconsciously new that his time was going to be very short and indeed it was as he ended up in an airplane disaster. One other last anecdote that I thought was comical was about a man driving a truck loaded with produce titled "30 Thousand Pounds of Bananas". This young fellow in a rush down a very steep incline ended up crashing the truck and all of its contents spewed forth. There is some sing-song type of lyrics that go with this song and its one of the more cheerful pieces that Harry often performed at his concerts. On one of my last trips to Anchorage I was going down the steepest grade of the whole highway system, namely Sheep Mountain, which at the end has a very sharp curve and to my amusement was an overturned truck with many people standing around I think picking up watermelons and I thought this was a strange coincidence again. Harry will probably always be with me in some sense and his music sits above my visor and I often plug it in and it never seems to get old. I had thoughts at one time to write a note to his wife and was going to try to get her address because I thought she would enjoy some of my commentary.

During Harry's concerts one of his promotional items was a poetry book that he had spent a good deal of time putting together and he often spoke of it and it was a compilation of a number of original poems and many of his lyrical stories. He sold it for the sole purposes of securing funds for his altruistic endeavors, namely the World Hunger Association. He talked about having sold as many as sixty thousand of these books and I began the search to see if I could come up with that book because I was enthralled with some of his storytelling. I went looking from Seattle to New York to Chicago and some of the other major book stores and could never find that book. One day I saw an old book store in Billings, Montana and walked in the door and wouldn't you know it, I found not only a copy of that poetry book but one that had been dutifully autographed so again the connections with Harry seems to be unceasing.

Two Cuties - Robe Lake, Valdez
Natalie

The Birthday Buck
11/19/2017

Throughout my career I was always looking for the big whitetail deer and we grew up in Minnesota and hunted in Wisconsin and even in the early days we seldom even saw an antler let alone an opportunity to see a large one. I think things have dramatically changed since the deer have adapted to the farm country and have flourished. However, that was not the case in my early days when there was only a one-day season. Treks up to the northern woods were seldom productive although we did manage a deer or so. Just seeing a trophy white-tailed buck is quite an accomplishment as they are very secretive and nocturnal in most cases as the have learned to stay hidden during the day and emerge late in the evening or during the night. The few cameras I put out for fun here in areas

Mother and big bear

of Wyoming showed that the two biggest deer showed up right after midnight where the does would show up at a much earlier time. In any event, I harken to say that on November 19, 2017, I reached my 75th birthday, which I still cannot fathom and I decided to spend that evening down in a creek bottom that I had previously scoped out. It was a neat little area with a creek on one side and a natural trail that ran parallel to the creek and I had made a small ground blind. As I took my seat early in the evening I stared up a trail and was amazed at this extraordinarily large white-tailed deer staring down from approximately one hundred yards and when they catch your presence they are gone in a flash but for whatever reason, maybe it had to do with the rut season, this particular buck just kept looking and proceeded to slowly walk my way. I had my archery equipment as the rifle season was over and of course the big issue was that the buck season had closed a few days earlier. That buck came in so close, even stopping by a bush momentarily which would have given me ample time to draw my bow and as if on cue he turned broadside and I was dumbfounded by the presence of this magnifi-

Last Christmas photo

cent critter and all I could do is enjoy his existence as he slowly walked by me. I don't think I will ever see that deer again but who knows. I still have access to this particular property that he is on and maybe day dream that I might have a chance at him, however I thought at least it was a neat experience to pass my birthday with.

Pops in Polar Bear Town

Long before Churchill, Manitoba became a tourist attraction for viewing polar bears somehow my father thought at the time that it would be a worthwhile trip to take the train to Churchill from Winnipeg and I think it had something to do with graduating from graduate school from the University of Manitoba. At that point Churchill had little notoriety for bears but there had been a couple incidents where people had been seriously hurt if not killed when bears would often get hung up on the mainland waiting for the ice to form. Since that time the number of bears has increased appreciably maybe having something to do with the global warming issue but it has become a major attraction for many a tourist and I'm sure a source of income for the locals. They've even constructed what they call "bear prison" because of the need to hold bears that are problematic in a safe zone pending their release into he wild. They have an actual bear patrol that watches the movement of the animals throughout the area and over time the bears have learned that the dump, etc. is the place to spend their time waiting for the ice flow to form.

The railroad trip to Churchill was an ordeal as I remember it took at least three full days to arrive at our destination. This particular train went through literally hundreds of miles of wilderness and it was the main source for moving supplies for the folks that lived in these remote areas. It seems like we stopped almost continuously and the trip took forever.

Rare picture inside Alaska Pipeline - George 1975

Biggest bear ever 30" skull record
Rick Ballow 1977

The bottom line of the trip was that we didn't see any polar bears but we were at least able to say that we saw Hudson Bay and we brought back an number of artifacts as gifts. This is probably one of the few trips that my father took as after returning back from World War II he rarely ventured far from home with the exception being with the help of my cousin, Kathleen, he drove a new pickup truck to Alaska and then got on the first airplane of his life to return to Minnesota. The only other trip that I can remember in my youth is one when we took his old Packard jalopy and found our way down to Florida where he wanted to meet up with a priest that he became quite involved with during World War II. The priest's name was Father Philbin and we found that he was living pretty high and mighty in a very large parish. The pictures I saw of him in my father's album was when he was saying mass in one of the remote islands and I know my father was endeared to him and I imagine they had many discussions about philosophy and theology. It just so happened that a famous hotel at the time was just completed building, namely the Fontainebleau, the premiere hotel in Miami at the time and he treated us to an exotic dinner that we were not accustomed to but it was a bit of a highlight of the trip. At the risk of being redundant, I always wish I would have taken more time with my dad and gathered some of his knowledge and experiences, specifically those that occurred during the war years. Youth and preoccupation with one's life, however seemed to preclude any interest in the matter and now its just too late. I do know that his trip to the Pacific was hellacious and I think at the time it took six or eight weeks in these huge troop ships where the sailors were stacked six or seven high bunks with most of them being sick most of the time and he mentioned the stench and heat of being incarcerated in these cargo holds. I can envision his great delight in returning home and I'm also guessing probably decided that he was never leaving home again after those three long years abroad.

Sabotage in Sand Point, Alaska

Sand Point is an island off the Alaskan Peninsula, probably three to four hundred miles west and south of Anchorage. I had made at least two trips to Sand Point and had planned another venture with my good friend George who at the time was living in Spokane following his time in the school districts in Alaska. I was hoping to show George some of the large bears that inhabit the area and at the time I know George drove almost non-stop from Spokane in order to make the trip. I previously arranged with the same gentleman that had taken us out previously, basically a commercial fisherman who was waiting for the salmon season to begin, he offered once again to take us out and drop us at some bay of our choosing. Sand Point is about five miles off of the mainland and it does take a sizeable craft to get to any of the mainland areas. On this particular trip I had shipped my Zodiac boat, motor and gear ahead of time which was not a cheap affair. We were on schedule and I remember us going to one of the local stores picking up odds and ends and I suspect that one of the local guides must have spotted us as being resident hunters who might be contemplating moving into one of his guide areas. In any event, the loading of all of our equipment was in itself an ordeal.

The Zodiac itself weighs well over one hundred pounds

Bob Peca, frequent partner
Sand Point Brown Bear

and the motor and gas, etc. makes for quite a haul of gear down the docks and into the larger fishing boat. After all of the preparations were made we were astounded to find out the following morning that the captain of the boat who was a local fellow advised us that we had to go see one of the native cooperation offices as someone had complained that we were crossing into native lands without permission. So with that we found our way up to the native office and were advised that in fact, if we wanted to go into any of the local bay areas we would have to pay fifteen hundred dollars per person just for the privilege of putting a tent on their property. They were very uncooperative in terms of offering us an alternative areas and indicated that they owned everything far and wide and really didn't give us the option of considering areas that were not covered by their territorial ownership. Even a trip to the BLM found us getting very poor information and we thought that somehow we were being shanghaied into a very untenable situation. To say we were disgusted was an understatement given the expense that we had already incurred such as the cost of the airplane right and the shipping of all of the supplies, etc. was well into the thousand dollar mark or beyond. With great disgust we began the arduous process of pulling all of our gear and were told that the next aircraft leaving would be a couple of days away, which further exasperated our situation. Of note was a young fellow who was working on the docks was gracious enough to give us some good information. He said "oh yeah, this is what they do to resident hunters and there are in fact areas you can go on without getting involved with the native trespass problem. He mentioned several bays that I kept in mind for future reference but at the point we had already committed to leaving. The native corporations have systematically begun to impose rules and regulations and at times charging enormous trespass fees even for fishing rights or anything for that matter. In fact, some of the permit areas on Kodiak Island are literally encapsulated by native properties and it's literally impossible to access them because of this issue.

In our frustration we spent the next several days licking our wounds and while we're waiting to board the aircraft back to Anchorage we had the good fortune to talk to another guide whose name eludes me at the point but he had been living in the area for many years and we explained to him how we had been systematically sabotaged and he generously offered to give us a ride someday into areas that would be out of the native areas and I thanked him for his generous offer and in fact ended up calling him a year or two later and sure enough he did take us into a really neat area, however that also ran into another guide's area

Last Moose - Husilia River
Post back surgery 2019

which created a situation that I do not want to get into at this point. However, it did involve him getting into some difficulties related to providing air taxi service without a license so again, this is comment on how competitive hunting has become particularly in the Alaska Peninsula area where there is such money involved and where the guides and natives are trying to maximize any exploitation of the situation. The next trip was indeed a more successful one, however there were some issues that made it very unpleasant, again related to a guide who protested our presence and even went to the point of having an attorney write us a letter saying that we had trespassed. This concludes my little story of some of the issues related to the commercialization of hunting in Alaska and I certainly have dealt with it first handedly as I have tried to convey.

The Toothless Mountain Lion

On or about January of 1998 I signed up to go on a mountain lion hunt with a fellow from Nevada. It turned out that it happened to be a renowned lion hound fellow who was currently living in Idaho, his name being Mike Young and I found out the he had been running cats for many years but did most of his hunting around a remote desolate area near Ely, Nevada. Indeed Ely is a stark area with miles and miles of nothing but barren ground desert country with some surrounding mountainous and rocky abutments.

It just so happens that when I arrived in Ely I discovered that Mike had buddied up with an old friend of his, namely a man named Dawson Riley. Riley was up in age but had spent his life in the business of hounds and cats. I soon realized that I was amidst some guys with years and years of experience and in some ways they ended up being competitive as they both had taken different junctures in the cat hunting business. I was soon to learn that cat hunting, be it mountain lion or whatever, is a very specialized affair and the jargon and the vernacular that goes along with hound hunting is indeed unique. Dawson in particular had wild stories of the time he spent in Belize, formally British Honduras, where he pursued jaguar in the jungle swamps of Belize, which is a nasty task for sure. There has been some renowned stories of cat hunting for jaguars in their prime and in fact I attended a seminar one time with a noted jaguar hunter that used hounds and a spear to impale the critters in the most blood thirsty enterprise that one would fathom. Without saying, the jaguars have been closely protected for many years and still remain one of the stealthiest of all of the wild cats that inhabit the bowels of South America. Many are still seen but for the most part are extremely elusive and are seldom captured on video of any sort. In any event, I was in the company of some gentlemen that had well over fifty years of experience in the cat industry and that in itself is an experience that I took in. I'm not sure why Dawson came to Nevada but I guess it was just part of his passion that he had not totally given up and somehow he hooked up with Mr. Mike Young to spend a month or two pursuing the local mountain lions in the northeast part of Nevada. The houndsman are indeed a unique group and they speak a jargon that is again unique to their craft and one finds himself truly an outsiders when it comes to participating in their discussion as the have their own lingo for most of the activity that occurs. Each of the hounds has a specific task, some are those that cut the track and the other ones actually tree the cat in the final stages of the chase. This is somewhat reminiscent of a bull fight and it's hard to understand the drama that does take place unless you are actively participating in it. So I again found myself in the midst of some gentleman that had devoted their life to a rather strange passion. The hounds that they used are indeed specialized critters, their ability to pick up scent is incredible and not explainable. There are some very exotic tales of bloodhounds, for example, that can pick up the most remote odors to track victims of abduction and there really is no plausible explanation for the unique abilities. As we traveled about, each of the fellows had their own hounds that were housed in small cubicles that were in their pickup trucks. Most of them were fitted with what they call mercury collars so that when they in fact had treed an animal, their heads would be up which trips the mercury switch which tells the houndsman that they in fact had a cat up a tree. The obvious predicaments is that they dogs could cover miles and miles of country, oftentimes going over mountain ranges and its only with GPS technology that they are able to recover their dogs which again could be miles away. Some of these specialty hounds are worth a lot of money and sometimes they did elude to the actual worth of these dogs and the training involved.

I arrived sometime after the first of January only to find out that the snow that had fallen earlier had already melted and this in itself created a situation because picking up a sign on dry land is completely different than hounds that can pick up a sign from dry conditions. Our day consisted of running the tops of mountain ranges usually on two-track lanes that covered miles and miles of nothingness, again our eyes were always peeled for any fresh track that we could discern. As with most predatory animals, tracking after a fresh snow is the optimal situation as everything seems to move after fresh snow which gives a predator the opportunity to find prey animals. Unfortunately, as the days wore on we only saw snow melting and nothing to look forward to in terms of fresh snow conditions. Several times we treed bobcats that I probably should have taken advantage of given their worth but I deferred that and focused on finding a mountain lion track that would be worth pursuing. This turned into a very arduous day of pounding roads and before I was done with this trip my neck was so constricted from holding it upright on the bumpy rutted roads that I could hardly move by the time I was done. We did find an occasional old track but it was interesting to watch the dogs stick their nose in each of

Ely, Nevada - ancient old female 20 yrs+

the tracks and the handlers could easily determine whether the dogs were vaguely interested in pursuing what they had found. Again, reading the dogs and their instincts was a distinctive talent that only someone with years of experience could analyze. The days dwindled on and at one point I found myself with Mr. Riley up on the high ridge bouncing along a two-lane rut and soon we found ourselves high centered in some rotten snow conditions which brought us to a halt. I could tell that he had little experience in snow conditions whereas I came from Alaska and was used to fighting these conditions. Somehow, after much manipulation and with the use of a jack to move the vehicle off of high center we were able to extract ourselves, however we would have been in a world of hurt if we had not been able to get loose as we were miles from anywhere and did not have the use of a cell phone or any way of communicating.

It seems that if my memory holds true that the evening before I was scheduled to leave I was with Mike Young and we were checking out some areas where at one point he had taken a snow machine and had taken off to check some trail areas and came back to tell me that in fact he had found some relatively fresh tracks. The following morning I was scheduled to leave but he felt we should return to this area and check it for any new fresh tracks. As it turned out that particular morning he took off with the snow machine and was back seemingly within the hour with a great deal of excitement saying he actually saw a cat that was making its way along the ridgetop, a sight that is seldom seen giving the elusive nature of the animal. So it was with a gust of exuberance that we jumped on the snow machine and took off to the hilltop and sure enough, the dogs had treed this particular animal in a very short distance. I remember jumping off the back of the snow machine and grabbing my archery equipment and heading towards the dogs who were yelping with excitement and sure enough, in the treetops was a cat staring down and moments later I found myself releasing an arrow and that cat tumbling out of the tree, stone dead. I was more than a little bewildered with the outcome. Usually the houndsman will tie the dogs up before you proceed to shoot at a cat in a tree as they know that if the cat has any life in it that it can do some serious damage to the dogs and in this case somehow the dogs got loose and they were quickly on top of the cat but they emerged unharmed because the cat was deceased. Even in my decrepit age, even at the time, I was able to put in a lethal shot that essentially took the animal down within seconds so I was relieved that I did not create a situation with his dogs that could have been very costly for sure. As it turned out, this particular cat was extraordinarily old and the teeth were in terrible condition. The canines were rounded off with large holes in them indicative of major dental condition and the biologist that checked it before we left aged it at around twenty year of age. He was amazed that the animal was still alive and thought that he probably survived by chasing jack rabbits as his canines were in such poor condition that he would be unable to kill a deer. As it turned out, the cat was quite emaciated but did have a large skull and did make the minimum for the record book for whatever that might be worth. Needless to say after such a hectic week of driving miles and miles with little result that was an enthusiastic end to a very long week. This animal eventually was mounted in a very impressive way laying on a log and is now somewhere in Florida in a gift store so it is still being admired for its worth. Certainly the cat mountain lion is a most impressive animal in many ways and if anyone has ever seen their tremendous speed it is mind boggling. On at least one or two occasions I have seen them come out of a tree and literally you can only see a brown flash as the speed is incredible. However, their downfall as with most of the big cats is their small lung capacity and their speed is very short lives which is where the dogs are able to tree them or corner them be it in North American or in Africa. I often think I would like to experience the mountain lion hunt again and have talked to a few gentlemen in Wyoming who actively pursue this endeavor and maybe I will still put this on my bucket list as it is truly a unique experience.

Ram Glacier

For those who haven't tracked the history of the National Park Service in Alaska it has gone from one extreme to the other. The State of Alaska is approximately seventy percent federally owned and there has been a long-standing battle regarding subsistence usage and the protection of the national parks and reserves. One of the significant conflicts involve the non-subsistence user, basically the sportsman, having access to federal lands and for years they battled back and forth with the federal government finally giving the state an ultimatum that if they did not come up with an acceptable subsistence priority use of the lands that they would in fact take control of all management on federal properties. This was never resolved to anyone's satisfaction and in fact, the federal people began imposing their own regulatory rules. During the Carter administration he issue an executive order and basically shut down huge parts of the state for any sport hunting, etc. It was very controversial and created the ire of most of the local people. As the park service began their regulatory invasion there were protests and threats of violence to the park service. Of specific interest to those living in our community was the access to the Wrangle Mountain area, which is historically something we used for all manner of outdoor activity. I remember going to town meetings where park service people would be in attendance and bare the wrath of the local people. They compromised the situation initially by giving temporary usage permits to those that could show that they had historically used the park area which included hundreds of thousands of square miles of area in the Wrangle St. Elis area joining up to the Canadian border. I in fact did manage to get a permit given the fact we had hunted in the area off and on for a number of years. The park service as noted was getting little if any help from the locals. They often wouldn't sell them gas and it was often an all out bitter relationship.

In our case we were particularly interested in accessing some of the premier sheep areas in the Wrangle Mountains, particularly in the Chitna area which in fact produced the number one sheep of all times as well as two or three others that were in the top ten of the record books. This area known for the genetics it was highly coveted in the days when guides were accessing the area. It is very rugged indeed with extremely high peaks and the glacier itself at least in the moraine area is something to tackle. The area that we were specifically interested in was the Ram Glacier drainage, which is where the famous Schwank head came from in 1964. Interestingly, the guide that took him in there was a fellow named Jack Wilson who lived in Glennallen and who subsequently moved to Valdez and opened a store. We were able to sit down with him and get the first-hand account of that hunt that produced the world record that still stands today. Mr. Schwank himself died some short years after in an airplane incident. Jack described in some detail how they accessed the area and of course at the time they could land very close to the entrance of the drainage. This was no longer possible with the new regulations from the park service as aircrafts were not allowed to land in the park and you had to literally walk in without the use of any motorized vehicles. Jack told us how to hunt the area as the drainage is sided by extreme steep precipitous slides that are difficult to climb even for the best. He told us not to even try but go situate yourself out on the glacier itself and eventually the rams will come down to an altitude that you can stalk

Rick Richter in his prime, heading out.

them. Unfortunately, we did not take his advice and it cost us dearly as things developed.

My partner at the time was Mr. Rick Rickter, a larger than life character who has spent many a year flying aircraft around the state and was our local banker and went on to open up a very successful commercial appraisal business in Anchorage. We took many a sheep hunt usually later in the season after labor day and met with some mediocre success, however he was game to give this a whirl and we found ourselves being flown in from McCarthy to Hubert Landing which is on the border of the park and from which we had to make our way into the glacier. Rick is for sure a very gregarious kind of guy who I think at one point in time probably knew every barkeep and person of interest in Anchorage. Being part of the flying community he knew all of the guides and lodges throughout the state. He was an ex-marine and spent his time in Vietnam and did suffer a serious leg wound that at times would effect his stability but it never slowed him down.

Rick and I had several eventful trips in the Wrangles prior to this effort on Ram Glacier but we never did score any large trophies, however Rick on his own did manage to come up with a large sheep out of the famous Tok management area. The area as noted around Ram Glacier and the whole Chitna valley is daunting. Not only do you have to fight the alders at the lower levels but then you get up into the extreme steepness of the mountains. In our case, we had to cross at a minimum of three glacier-fed streams that were torrents at the time. One in particular held us up for at least a day or two as the current was so extreme and we had to wait until the early mornings when things would cool off and the water current would subside to a degree. So, after a good two and a half days of arduous walking we made our way to the opening of the famous Ram Glacier where we setup a base camp. As we pondered the area it was obvious that the area was extremely rugged with the moraine itself being full of large crevasses and running water. I know those that have landed on the glacier in earlier days would land up very high and then the walking would be considerable better but without the ability to take in an aircraft you had to start from the very bottom of the glacier which is where the rugged area begins. After setting our camp up we started the trek up the Ram Glacier drainage itself and within a relatively short time we could see rams situated in high precipitous cliffs and seemed very comfortable to just sit there as they were in full command of the view and we could see that it would be very difficult to climb to their level. We did try on a number of occasions but area was fraught with shale slides so that every step you took you seemed to slide back two and it became crystal clear that what Jack Wilson had told us about trying to climb up to where the sheep were was going to be a real issue. Nonetheless we continued to plunder around as best we could and ended up climbing up an area that we could physically manage. When we crested the mountain we sat there for some time and low and behold a herd of probably twelve rams were making their way up the steep hill to where we were situated. The last sheep in the line was the larger of the bunch and I took the shot and as it turned out, I should have waited another thirty seconds to have made sure that he had cleared

The Famous Ram Glacier, home of the world record.

the edge. With that, the sheep tumbled backwards and literally disappeared from sight as we surveyed the situation it was clear that the sheep had in fact tumbled the entire length of the steep precipice and was somewhere down in the drainage. With that we were faced with an attempt to recover that animal and that involved us going completely down the mountain and circling around to the adjoining drainage where we thought that the animal would somehow be laying. As it turned out, sure enough we found the sheep in a deplorable condition. He was literally pummeled with muzzle crushed in and his limbs were damaged badly and there was no salvageable meat that we could find. Fortunately, the horns themselves that were not that large were not broken but they should have been given the several thousand feet that the critter had fallen. So all that we were left with was the horns and we were sure to take pictures of the damaged carcass as not bringing out salvageable meat is a serious offense. The following day we found ourselves back in our base camp and sitting exhausted from our efforts of the previous day and sure enough as predicted, down came a small band of very large rams that actually went onto the glacier itself and again, we should have heeded Mr. Wilson's advice to setup a camp on the glacier itself as we would have had access to those magnificent critters. While we were on the glacier there was remnants of old tents and it was in fact the way the area was hunted years ago. Our time was running short so we just shook our heads in disappointment and did leave a cache of supplies in hopes that we might return the following year and do it right this time. The next day or two found us stumbling back and crossing those God awful streams and finally arriving at Hubert's Landing. There we had left a precious cache of freeze dried food and some other supplies and as not unexpected, they were totally torn apart by one of the local grizzly bears. There was absolutely nothing left. That bear even punctured holes in the gas can and ate a whole case of freeze dried food which

I'm sure would have blown up his belly at some point. So we were surely beaten by the Ram Glacier experience but at that time were still looking to the future for another go around now that we knew what was to be expected and how possibly to hunt it more successfully.

On our return flight to Gulkana we were met by my wife Judy and her good friend Suzy Collins who unfortunately passed away recently and was a wonderful person. I'm sure we blurted out our tale of woe and missed opportunity and they took it in with their usual lack of interest in our exploits I'm sure.

As expected, but with great disappointment, the park service systematically revoked our permits the following year. This was their sly way of placating the locals with the original permits in hoping to quell the antagonism and they now had put into place their original plan to exclude all of those people who wanted to hunt the area with the only exception being permits given to those who actually live a subsistence lifestyle in the catchment area. I recall going back to talk to Mr. Wilson and he just kind of shook his head and I remember him saying, "Well, at least you guys had a chance to see where the world record came from". Sometimes later I believe he wrote a book of his guiding experiences called "Glacier Wings and Tales". I have not read that book but it would be interesting to take a look at it and I'm sure he recounted his expedition with Mr. Schwank. I believe Jack died not many years after this experience but I think that the family still operates a liquor store business in the Glennallen area.

The Tale of the Lynx

The lynx in Alaska is one of the most mystical critters that I encountered in my time there. The lynx are prolific in a good part of Alaska and in a great part of Canada. Their pelts have been highly coveted for years and the prices have varied for years and I know at one point reached well over five hundred dollars. In recent times they have lost some of their value whereas the other spotted cats such as the bobcat of the northern states remain high in demand and I suspect the demand comes from China. Most of the spotted cats are highly protected around the world. The Alaskan lynx is indeed a beautiful creature with their large yellow eyes and their huge feet and luxurious silver hair that is extraordinary. They are built for speed with long legs and snowshoe-like feet allow them to run on the top of some of the softest snow conditions as they pursue their primary prey, the snowshoe hare. They entire life-cycle is dependent on the snowshoe rabbit and as their population declines so does the lynx population. In my last few years of trapping in Alaska the lynx and rabbit population were at a very low level.

Over the years I did make a number of efforts to catch lynx but never had the time to go up into the areas where they were more prolific which was in the interior and I did

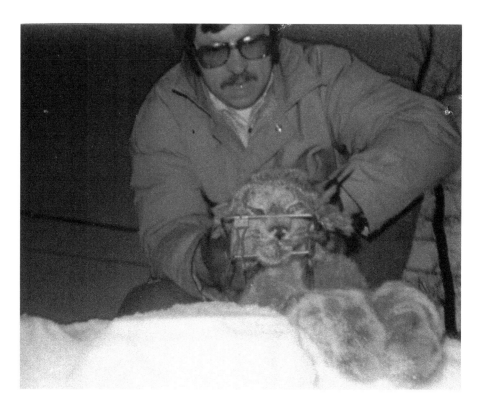

Freak catch wtih tiny martin trap - George May

not have the time or means to drive up there except for the weekends and its unfair to leave a leg-hold trap that long without being attended to. With one notable exception during the early days of our trapping efforts we made a phenomenal catch of a lynx that was indeed unique. My good friend George Maykowskyj and I were putting some traps along the pipeline prior to its being built and made a number of martin sets and a few wolverine sets. For those not familiar with martin trapping I would use what they call a body grip trap, which results in the quick demise of the animal and is very humane in that respect. The actual circumference for the size trap for a martin is very small, not more than six inches by six inches and it forms a perfect square that you place in a box baited on a tree limb. One day when we were checking our sets to our amazement was a lynx laying on the ground stone dead and to our utter astonishment the lynx had put his nose into the box and the trap caught him around the nose and somehow the lower bar had caught him under his jawline, I guess enough to cut off his airways. This was indeed a rare occurrence and I should have submitted a picture to someone who would have appreciated how unusual this was.

On that same particular night where we had this rare catch of a lynx we also found a wolverine in our traps and it was one that had literally harassed us for days on end going from set to set and usually stealing any bait and or martins that had been caught. Wolverines are noted for following snowshoe trails and he was obviously delighted in being fed with these sets that we had left. So that was one of our more glorious evenings and we had caught the wolverine that had plagued us for so many weeks.

The lynx while not particularly hard to catch finding where they move and analyzing their travel patterns is always to the key to being successful. They will often follow creek bottoms but they are found almost exclusively where the rabbit population is plentiful. Following my retirement I spent more than a little time driving over the infamous Thompson Pass and trapped along the road areas as I did not use a snow machine as most of the serious trappers did. Trapping on a road system is not much fun most of the time as does have a lot of competition but I was not in the position to take off on a snow machine by myself as it can get you in some dire straits and I thought at the time it was not wise to do so. I knew that there were several serious trappers in the area and tried my best to avoid going where the were knowing my presence would not be well-received. I did however, manage to catch a few beautiful cats over the years and it was always the highlight of the year as you would approach these critters it was with mixed feelings as they are so beautiful and it is bittersweet when you actually have to dispatch them. However, in this case I was advised by one of the local biologists that lynx in the area that I was working in were in dire straits and would probably starve eventually given the rabbit population.

During one of my last years of trapping the road system I decided I was not going to use any leg hold traps because it was so difficult to get up to the area when road conditions where bad. So I relied almost exclusively on snares because this would dispatch the animals but it also presented great difficulties as it was hard to find suitable areas where there were sufficient rabbits to successfully use snares. However, I did persist and this eventually created a situation that I thought was worth recounting. In one area I had put two different cubby type sets surrounded by snares approximately two miles apart and each time that I would arrive I was finding that a lynx had come through the area and had taken the bait and had somehow managed to avoid all of the snares that I had placed in the surrounding area. This happened with both of the sets that I had and it continued for seemingly at least a month. It became apparent that I in fact was feeding this animal and he was living off of the bait that I had left usually hanging them from a limb or in a cubby type of area as lynx are very visual and they often will pick up anything that is moving and one would often leave a wing to float in the breeze. My frustration with this particular cat grew and I finally brought along James Wade who quickly appraised the situation, as he always does, and he noted that there was some drag marks that he perceived and we concluded that in fact this animal must be dragging some type of trap on his foot. The amazing part of this was that he was able to move this trapped foot and avoid the snares moving from one bait set to another. We even went to the point of putting up a camera device that was motion censored to see how that cat was so expertly avoiding the snares that I had laid. As I approached the last week of trapping season I concluded that I had to do whatever it took to catch this cat as he was obviously going to be dying of starvation, particularly if he was hurt and impaired. With that I set a number of leg hold traps on both of the adjoining sets and sure enough the last day of the season there he sat staring with a very substandard leg hold trap around his toes that were badly damaged. The poor animal had obviously been hurting for some time so it was bittersweet that we were able to put him out of his misery. I would estimate that I made at least ten trips or so during those last few weeks which would be somewhere around a thousand miles of driving all for the sake of catching this poor animal. I don't think I caught another lynx after this situation but felt that

Last cat of my career

I ended my lynx trapping in a honorable way if that would be acceptable comment given the inherent cruelty of the trapping particularly with leg hold devices.

I recently completed a mounting of two lynx together, one being a smaller female that had all white toes which was very unusual and the larger male cat standing over it and I thought that the piece itself was quite stunning.

Mink Mania

Throughout my many years in Valdez I spent more than a little time catching mink. The area is truly covered by a myriad of creeks and streams that flow from the mountains into the flats and then eventually into the ocean. With the amount of fish that go up these creeks the foraging for subsistence for these critters and many others is abundant. All manner of critter live off of the salmon that come up these streams by the thousands. Not much is left by the time winter arrives. The eagles, crows, ravens, coyotes, otters and any other creature will feast on the carcasses of these salmon that often times go up many miles of creek bottom and can be found in some cases as late as November and even December.

My mink trapping involved mostly the area around Robe

River which is one of the major rivers that come out of Robe Lake and makes it's way approximately six or seven miles down into the ocean. It happened to be close to my home and in fact was for ten years, on my property edge and made it very accessible for my trekking about. I had several favorite haunts where I would make sets often with a variety of baits and one being the culvert area that the highway crossed and the other area was where a large tree had fallen and it had created a natural cubby. Most people in Valdez wouldn't have a clue to the amount of critters such as otters and mink that make their way up and down the river and you often seldom even see a mink track as they spend most of their time in the water and are abundantly fed with the remains of the salmon. In the two particular sets I had worked them religiously for a number of years and my success rate was at times almost one hundred percent. It seemed that almost every time I checked a trap there would be a mink in it and I had made it such that the animal would drown very quickly in the current as I staked the trap out in deeper water. The mink would head for water in a pond and be caught underwater and would essentially be unmarked when I recovered it. I harken to think of the many trips, in the hundreds for sure, that I made down the trails to my various little spots often accompanied by a few friends and for sure my granddaughter who used to go with me on many treks. It was wonderful therapy for me as it took a bit of arduous work when snow was deep particularly when there was a new snow fall covering even a few hundred yards would find you totally exhausted. After the trail was beaten down, obviously things improved appreciable but the hanging alders always created issues as you went along the trail and they would vary from day to day as the snow would continue to push the alders down and it would require clearing as you went. I would hate to think of the number of mink that I caught in my career but I would think it would be in the hundreds and it was sufficient enough to make several coats. I know I adorned my poor mother with a wonderful shawl that that is now owned by my cousin and I made God knows how many hats, etc. from their hides. Coastal minks are not as prized as those in the interior but nonetheless they are wonderful fur animals and have been trapped for millenniums. The fur prices for mink have hardly varied over the last hundred years. When I pick up one of the old-fashioned magazines dating into the 1920s where the price of mink, even in those days, was fetching up to twenty dollars or more. I missed those mornings when I would make my way through familiar paths and always with great expectation that at the end of it would be a wily mink in the water, often requiring me to pull myself down a rather precipitous bank and with a long hook and in my case it was a long ice axe I would retrieve the critter and take it back to the shop for proper handling.

Late in 2013 I recall one of the more amazing experiences

A pile of mink and martin, many from backyard

with the snow conditions that I feel is worth recounting. As the snow falls in Valdez, it progressively pushes down the alders that often stand as high as twenty feet and essentially you are walking on a bed of crushed down alders which makes the going good in some ways but not so much when you find air pockets between the branches where your snowshoe falls into these and at times you have great difficulties extracting your foot from five to ten feet of snow cover. Along the bank of the river there was relatively tall alders that would often be bent and at times this would create a great problem as you would have to pull your way through this and it formed a fence-like abutment that made it very difficult to say the least. I spent a thousand mornings cussing out the alders and the devil's club that made venturing so miserable. On one particular March day we had received well over six feet of snow and I found my way trekking though waist high fresh show and as I approached where I thought the bank of the river was everything looked completely different and here I had been at this same spot hundreds of times. What had occurred as I discovered was that they alders had bent forward over the bank of the river and had created a cornice of snow and I was not able to discern the bank, which in itself is a good five foot drop down to the river, and as I trekked along I found myself over the top of the river approximately a good ten feet above the river and I was astonished that I had not broken through which would have created quite a tumble into the river. How I missed not picking up where I was at was mind boggling and I carefully back tracked across this cornice to the point where I thought the bank was and began digging my way down to the edge of the bank and finally down to the river when I finally slid down the hole I looked up and said, "My Lord, I'm ten feet down!" and it was kind of an eerie feeling and it just so happened that on that particular day I not only had a mink in the trap but also an otter and then had the predicament of digging myself out of this hole to get out of this entrapment that I found myself in. Fortunately I always carry my trusty ice axe so I made a number of steps and little by little I pulled myself up and up until I could get ahold of an alder at the top of the bank and pull myself, my gear and my critters out. I remember I had the where-withal to have called my good friend Stephen Goudreau and told Steve that I was stuck in a hole and had a heck of a time dragging myself back out and I think he reluctantly made his was out as he was always so generous with his willingness to help and I did meet him halfway down the trail dragging all of my gear and the two critters that I had just caught. It was a strange phenomenon that I had never experienced and given my time in that particular spot I was still shaking my head as to how I got myself in that predicament. It would have ended rather poorly if in fact I had broken through that snow and tumbled into the river and although the water is not deep its certainly full of protrusions and rocks and I suspect I could have hurt myself.

So this is the end of my mink mania story but it was some-thing I did with great passion and it occupied a tremendous amount of time and it gave me an excuse to make my way along familiar trails and always everyday there was some-thing new to observe such as an eagle or an otter or whatev-er. It was something that I truly miss now that I find myself in Wyoming where water and snow conditions are certainly not even close to what I had experienced for so many years.

Bulawayo or Bust

Sometime in the early 1980's I had the brainstorm to do an Africa trip and at that time the prices were considerably different than what they are today. If one stuck to the plains game one could go for a remarkably cheap price somewhere in the one fifty to two hundred dollar a day range whereas now the hunts are going for well over a thousand or more. I got the name of a gentleman in Zimbabwe who was basically starting out his guiding business, named Clive Lennox. I had originally talked to my good friend Walter McGehee who I had dragged into a few dangerous situations but after putting a deposit down he thought better of this venture and the idea of going internationally was something he did not want to cope with. However, at the time I was much more gung-ho than I found myself in later years and I put together some money for the most part it was tax returns from mounted critters donated to the school district. In those days the IRS was very liberal in acknowledging donations even to the extent of including total replacement of the hunt cost which they soon altered and at this time it is very closely monitored and scrutinized. At the time however, it did generate enough money for me to justify taking this trip. Somehow I talked myself into the trip as I often do and usually its with the philosophy of that if I don't do it now I will kick myself later when I don't have the wherewithal and this has been my rationale in many of my crazy trips over the years. In any event, I found myself booking a hunt with Mr. Clive Lennox of Bulawayo, Zimbabwe. Bulawayo is one of the larger cities in Zimbabwe, the capital being Harare. He had recently just opened his guiding business and I would guess he was in his late twenties and I was not much older than that. I found out that Clive had recently just finished his tour of duty in the Rhodesian Army and the Rhodesian War had gone on for approximately ten years as the local black population was aspiring to detach them- selves from the colonialism that had prevailed in most of the African countries. If my history is accurate, Zimbabwe, formerly known as Rhodesia, was a colonial possession of either England or the Netherlands. Most of the white folk

Zimbabwe are seemingly English or Dutch. Clive himself, I believe was of Dutch origin but had grown up in South Africa and had moved to Zimbabwe and joined the military. At that point the black control of the government was just taking form and a fellow name Joseph Mugabe was now the primary dictator of the country and of interesting note he remained in power until as recently as 2018. As I understand, he was finally dethroned at the age of ninety-three or ninety-four and he was a bit of a notorious dictator and the country itself has been poorly managed since the black control took power. The white population was somewhere in the one or two percent, however as in most colonial countries they occupied and owned most of the property and the blacks were relegated to a very low level of subservience. One does not get a real understanding of this until you see it in person. The conditions are deplorable and reminiscent of what the slavery situation was in the South during the pre-civil war days.

I found myself making a solo trip to Zimbabwe itself a daunting experience as I was soon to find out. Just a few months before my departure there was a major incident that occurred very close to Bulawayo where a tour bus was captured and the occupants were never found with at least two gentlemen from Seattle that were missing when I arrived. A competing tribal organization that had been unsuccessful in competing with the Mugabe regime were still in a guerilla warfare and plundered the countryside. Anyone going to Africa finds themselves landing in Johannesburg, South Africa and finding your way through that maze of humanity is often a bit unsettling as the confusion and disorganization is obvious. The long lines with people speaking many languages and there seems to be no semblance of order. This was particularly true as white officials were being replaced by black folk that were obviously not equipped to do the job. You could tell in their manner and in their organization that they truly did not have a clue what they were doing but had been giving the job. There is a lot of history about Zimbabwe that I'm not fully knowledgeable about but I know it included the Boer War that occurred sometime in the nineteenth century where locals had broken away from English control and there's a lot of detail that I should be more familiar with but I was not, however Clive did give me a bit of a history lesson that I did try to take in at the time. Clive himself was a Colonel and I could tell by his demeanor and manner that he was used to giving orders and he ran his camp in a very regimented fashion but his confidence was also very evident in all that he did. His dealing with the black locals also very apparent and he dealt with them as servants and truly you felt like you were in the old south. I think that the whites, for the most parts, viewed the blacks as less than human and treated them accordingly.

Clive was certainly good company and that time he was a youthful fellow with great energy and enthusiasm. All of his equipment was meticulously cared for and he made it a point to tell me that he did all of the work on his vehicles himself and you could tell that he was most serious about his enterprise. Most of the stuff in Zimbabwe had been taken over by large cattle ranches which for the most part, systematically over time, moved all of the indigenous wildlife out of the area as they grazed the ground to the point where the indigenous wild animal had nothing to eat and they disappeared and also I'm sure they were exploited for their meat and consumed by the local population. The introduction of cattle in Zimbabwe and particularly in South Africa have been major obstacles to the continuation of wildlife that had been there for millennium. It has been the safari business that has created the funds and has put value on these wild creatures and have actually been the catalyst for restoring the populations in many areas. If there was not money value attached to them they would certainly not be there. In some areas, particularly in South Africa, the elephants and all manner of plains game have been restored to the area as they have managed ranches for that exclusive purpose funded by out of country money. So the incongruity of killing critters for money has in fact resulted in conserving the population and this became crystal clear as I gained a fuller understanding of what had transpired over the years. Left to their own designs, every animal in Africa would be killed and we saw that in person with the amount of poaching that occurs in most of the country. Without the institution of some of the park areas and the management that has occurred from the hunting business, Africa would have no semblance of the Africa that has been conjured up in the minds of people that view it as a wild and untouched place. Poaching still is a major issue in many of the national parks, however the government in many of the countries have organized anti-poaching patrols that have had controlled a good deal of the poaching, however that is still a prevalent problem particularly with such species and rhinoceroses which have great value for their horns. In South Africa in particular and I believe in other countries they have gone so far as to anesthetize these animals and cut their horns off so they no longer have inherent value. Even though the Rhodesian war was over and the black population was technically in control it was still very evident that the whites were in control and managing most of the government and particularly in the rural areas. All of the ranches had black help there were housed in very substandard condition and again were treated in a more of a slave-like fashion than one would expect. Mugabe was the prime minister for so many years and was closely affiliated to a lot of the communist countries in the hemisphere including Gaddafi of Libya and a number of other Russian backed countries that were still prevalent in the Cold War era.

I had one other gentleman in camp, a fellow from Georgia that stuck out in my mind and he was a rather distasteful character if I remember and his southern bias came out in a number of ways particularly as he referred and treated the blacks that were working for Clive. In one instance, one of the skinners mishandled one of his critters and he

took great delight in berating this poor fellow. There is definitely a pecking order in the Safari business. The lead man being the white, professional hunter and the second in command would be the tracker whose skills are such that it leaves one shaking their head. The trackers are selected for their expertise and finding the most minute sign of animals and or situations where they are wounded and they have to track them. I know that they take a great deal of time to pick the right personnel for this position and they often work their way up the ranks. The lowly ones being the skinners and those that do other camp chores. The trackers come from the rural areas where they have done this activity for millenniums and they have almost an uncanny sense of the grounds they survey and they can not explain how the can see things that no one else could have and they have the most refined sense of what is there. They can see a bent over piece of grass in the dry sands and tell you which direction that particular animal was going. They can tell you that the animal is hit in a certain spot given what they see in terms of drag marks or anything that gives them clues to what is occurring with them and they can often see things that no one else can see and the truly are remarkable in their expertise. After spending some time in these conditions and this being my first trip to Africa, one can only feel guilty and I progressively felt this more so as the trip continued. The clothing that these people use is for the most part tattered and most of them run around with no shoes and before the trip was over and I know I gave away almost everything I own to them and I felt guilty enough later on to have sent a whole box of shoes and other items back to the camp and whether they ever received them or not, I do not know.

I had a very limited list of animals that I was interested in pursuing and most of it was dictated by my limited resources. At that time the trophy fees which are government fees was extremely low compared to what I see going on these day and, for example, a sable which is one of the most aristocratic of all the antelope is priced well into the four to five thousand dollar range where I think I paid six hundred dollars for the government fee. I think my entire trip was somewhat less than seven thousand dollars and this would easily be tripled now. One of the first animals I took was in fact a sable, which is a magnificent animal with sweeping horns, and his black and white striped hide is stunning. Fortunately, I made some decent shots as one must pay the trophy fee if an animal is wounded and not recovered. I had the use of my good friend, John McCune's trusty 375 H&H that had been modified by his brothers and it seems to be on automatic every time the trigger was touched. It was extraordinarily accurate and I don't think

I missed a shot except in one instance.

I took a number of animals on this trip but probably the one that struck my interest most and put some fear of God in me was that of the Cape buffalo. We tracked a small herd of buffalo and they would pick up our scent and would be moving through the high brush and when they would spook the ground would rumble and it truly gave one a sense of being at the low end of the food chain. We approached this particular herd several times with no success and finally found myself face to face with a bull, not of course the most idea position for a shot but I took it anyways and to my utter amazement the animal went completely back up on his hind legs and went upside down impaling his horns into the ground, leaving us all a bit shaken. The bullet had entered through the brisket area and we found it true enough embedded in the spinal cord, which accounted for his quick demise. A wounded buffalo is something that is highly feared by even the most seasoned professional hunter and there is more than a few guides and sometimes hunters that are killed each year in Africa because of their encounters with the awesome buffalo that sometimes knows no fear, particularly if wounded. There was a few occasions that we were face to face with the herd of buffalo and it came to mind that if they did charge there wasn't a tree in sight that could have been climbed and we could have easily met a fate of being trampled as once they start their run there's nothing that seems to get in their way and they crush everything in their way as they go helter-skelter through the brush. Some of the more frightening aspects of this particular trip had more to do with the marauding political groups that were still trying to establish themselves a following a cessation of open warfare. We found ourselves in at least one ranch house and I sat with some astonishment as they setup a machine gun complete with tripod on the kitchen table. All of the help were brought into the compound and the fence closed each evening. Any questions I made about it were basically put off as they did not want to create any sense of fear among their patrons although I think the fear was well founded. As we made our way around the local countryside it became apparent that many of the local ranches had already been abandoned out of fear of the guerilla groups that were wandering and pillaging the area as they went. I was told by Clive that many of the older ranchers had given up the ghost on their property even though they had been there for years and had moved into the cities not wishing to deal with the obvious fears of being attacked or killed. This has continued to happen in the last thirty years and I had the occasion to return to Zimbabwe in 2001, another story to be told, but at the point I was given an updated history of the fact that the government is now methodically displacing all of the white ranchers and putting black folk, often those that come from the bush areas, in control of these ranches. The whites are given little if any notice and have lost their entire life work and it is of grave concern. Clive himself I know had purchased another piece of property and had revitalized it after much work and effort even to the point of seeing indigenous creatures such as elephants and a number of other endangered species move onto the property as he had allowed the natural habitat to regrow which drew in the indigenous animals that have now flourished there. At the risk of going into another story I was able, after twenty-eight years, to return to hunt with Clive although he had tapered his operation to a very small one and had restored a ranch as noted. During those twenty-eight years he had in fact been a major operator specializing in all of the "big five" animals and had done it all I think to the point of being burned out from the rigors of managing such an operation. He seemed to have gotten much more serious in his outlook on things and did confide in me that his younger brother who was a bit of a wild man as a remember and truly looked the picture of a true bush character had passed away, I suspect from over-imbibing that I think was a part of the rituals that they participate in as guides. Clive seemed to have gotten more conservative and at times I could sense some increased irritability about all manner of things that we did on the trip. The second venture was more directed at hunting leopard, which is a very specialized hunt, and the one that would in itself require some storytelling. Clive certainly is an interesting gentleman and I met his now wife but at the time of my first trip she was his girlfriend and I was told that he had several children now that had left the home. Periodically I used to hear from Clive when he would come to the various safari conventions looking for clientele but I have not heard from him in some time. On my first venture I was indeed awestruck but the whole

African venue and the cultural disparities of a third world country. One final little scenario included my leaving the country and at the point of customs, three black gentlemen took me into a back room and I thought for sure I was not going to see the airplane ride that I was expecting. They had obviously taken their positions to a point where they were going to extract as much money as they could from anyone that they had control of and essentially took all of the funds that I had in my pockets and were taking advantage of their new power position for sure. I was indeed relieved to board the aircraft on my way home. I can still see that airplane sitting on the tarmac and it was reminiscent of some of the movies that you see when I felt the increasing panic grow as I was being held somewhat in a captive situation not knowing what to expect but thinking the worst. I know for a time people where being discouraged from making trips to Zimbabwe and I think there are still some prohibitions that are of concern. In my last venture over there in 2001 I knew that many of the people on the aircraft were on their way to doing some type of safari thing and all of them with the exception of one small group would not go back to Zimbabwe. I think things have settled down some since then but it is apparent that the country is still in turmoil and I know Clive expressed to me in 2001 that he could at any time be given notice to evacuate his beautiful property that he had spent so much time revitalizing. However he did also insinuate that he had some inside connections, probably government officials that he had been connected with and felt more secure than many of his neighbors did. Africa is indeed a worthwhile thing to experience and I have a couple other stories that I could get into, one being in the northern Transvaal of South Africa where I found myself one of the DeBeers Diamond mine concessions which is a huge piece of property surrounding their diamond operation and that in itself was a story worth telling. Some of my mounts still have been retained but for the most part they have been sent off to auction despite my efforts to keep them restored and in good shape. Of note, African mounts have very little value and those that were sent off to auction in recent times fetched a very small amount and certainly didn't reflect the cost and the effort that went into securing them. At the point I don't think I will go into my other African stories although the leopard situation was one that still sticks in my mind and was truly quite an experience to see such an elusive cat in his natural environment.

Gold in the Black Spruce

One of the very unique critters that I've always been intrigued with for the many years I was in Alaska was the elusive pine martin. The pine martin is a cousin of the famed Russian sable that is truly worth its weight in gold. The Russian sable coats I suspect are worth thousands of dollars and essentially it is the same animal but I think that the cold weather and whatever other conditions that might cause it to have a fur quality that's probably superior to the North American martin. The pine martin is part of the weasel family and comes shortly after that of the mink, the youngest cousin of the weasel family is the weasel and there are several sub species of weasels in North America and in Alaska. The next in line would be the fisher, which is very akin to the martin except that it's

double in size and is primarily in the lower 48, mostly in the northern states, certainly in Canada and seems to be quite prominent in the northeast part of the states such as Maine or New Hampshire. The largest and most voracious of the weasel family is of course the wolverine which of course is a critter that is still highly sought after and one I spent a great deal of time trying to catch. I was successful on a number of occasions to catch the wily and nomadic wolverine but even the best of trappers only catch a few every year as they are very unpredictable in their movement although once they have a territorial trail they often will make the same loop in ten days or two weeks. Often they are found above the tree line and only come down when the snow conditions become such that they cannot navigate.

In any event I spent a good part of my days, particularly after my retirement, in trapping martin. They are the cash crop for the interior trapper and the prices have in recent times skyrocketed to an all time high, some well over one hundred dollars which is unheard of. What makes the martin so unique is that you never know that they are really around and they are quite nocturnal in their movements often spending their time in high ridge top areas usually in the heavy spruce where their primary prey animal is the squirrel. They are extremely fast and are great climbers. The other unknown factor of the pine martin is their movement because oftentimes they will disappear from an area and not be seen for a number of years and then they will somehow miraculously appear. The state of Alaska at some point did an extensive study of them using radio collars to find out what their true lifestyles were and there was little information to explain how they come and go from certain areas. The martin is a very curious critter and is easily trapped as it doesn't seem to have any wariness of a baited trap site, however finding out their locations is always the challenge. They often seem to run on high ridgelines and cover miles and miles it seems looking for prey. At one point I seldom could find a martin track in the Valdez area and then all of a sudden one year I started finding sign and was successful in catching quite a number of these beautiful animals. Their colors will very often from a very dark chocolate brown to those that are a blondish and have a lot of different variations in their color tones. Those that fetch the highest price were the dark colored males and there is quite a differential in price between those martins that come from the interior versus the coastal martins. Obviously the weather conditions are conducive to getting a more well-furred animal.

I always associate the martin with a miniature fox given its very prominent ears and its pointy nose. Their large feet are designed to cover miles and miles of snow country and they are just what I call a "neat" animal. Everything about them is intriguing and they even smell good. I often would put my nose in their deep fur and there is a wild freshness about them that gives way to their environment of being in the timber. At times I would go up and over into the interior and was successful in catching some fur but most of my time was spent locally around Valdez in a few little catchment areas where they seemed to run a certain territorial line, again usually on ridge tops. All of this required a great amount of energy of course particularly in the Valdez Valley where the snow was always deep and one would challenge your legs and lungs to snowshoe to the tree line where the martins would have greater potentiality of being in the area. Over the years I think I made at least two coats out of martin and they are luxurious furs for sure. I made quite a number of scarves for the various members of the family and cousins and my daughter to this very day wears her martin scarf to work as it provides great warmth and a bit of class to her attire. Of all the critters in Alaska, the martin is always prominent in my mind and I truly miss being out in the solitude of the forest that they reside. I have almost exclusively used box traps with body gripped traps called Conibear which are very humane. The northern trappers almost exclusively

Trapping partner, Krista

use leg hold traps on running poles where the pour critter ends up hanging after being caught but the cold of the interior quickly results in their demise. This would not be the case in the coastal areas where the warm weather would not be conducive to a humane end to their lives so for me it was always the Conibear trap that I could use and did not have to worry about checking as frequently as what would be required of a leg hold trap. The problem of course being that the squirrels in the area would often get even with their arch enemy and on more than a few occasions when I did not get back to a set that the local squirrels would come in and chew away at the hair of the martin and render it worthless. Also, left unattended, mice in the area would do significant damage. Martins do exist in our current environment in the Wyoming mountainous areas but I have not pursued them at this point in time and can only reflect back on the many days that I did spend snowshoeing into the mountainous slopes with great expectation that I would find gold at the end of the rainbow.

One of the very final days of my martin trapping I took along my friend Stephen Goudreau who always seemed to have brought me good luck and this day was no exception as we pulled the last of my sets and all had martin and one in particular was the largest martin I had ever seen and for some reason it was just plain huge. His head, his body, his feet, everything about him was extraordinarily large. The measurements of a martin can almost be predicted as the length of their nose to the base of their tail is usually in the seventeen to nineteen inch range where this one I think was somewhere close to twenty-two inches so there was no plausible reason for it's great size but it truly was a monster and a fitting end to my martin trapping career. This particular martin I handled very delicately and have preserved it in a life-size pose and I admire it almost daily as I walk by. So ends my tale of the gold in the black spruce, probably never to be repeated again and I viewed this with some degree of sadness.

The Last Hurrah!

This represents the last chapter of my little travelogue although I can think of a few other ventures that may have been worth recording. Somewhere around 2018 or before I kept telling myself that I should do one more that I should do one more venture someplace while I still was able to ambulate, knowing that my legs weren't getting any stronger for sure. This also coincided with the sale of several major taxidermy pieces that did bring in some sizeable returns although not as much as expected. One ironically happened to be a Siberian brown bear that I had taken a number of years ago and the mount itself was quite good I thought but it was sent out of country and it took a good deal of immigration and customs papers to accomplish that miracle. In any event, I started looking at several options and always wanted to go back to Kodiak Island where I had spent so much time and had never had an opportunity to take a really big bear. I had corresponded with one of the old-time outfitters who advised me that he had just sold his concession to one of his assistant guides and recommended his operation. The area was located in the west end of Kodiak where some of the biggest bears have come from over the many years. The famous guides of Olga Bay, namely Pinnell and Talifson. Those individuals were the premier guides of the 1950's and 60's and at one point they had taken the majority of the biggest bears ever to come off of Kodiak. They wrote several books that are indeed interesting to look through. When the cost of hunts were fifteen hundred dollars and it was really a fair-chase operation as there was no use of airplanes, etc.. Their clientele included a number of famous athletes, one of which I remember was Sam Snead, one of the most famous golfers of the century. I did finally book a hunt with the outfit that had taken over the area but unfortunately there were no fall hunts available and I knew enough that a spring hunt would include considerable climbing and I questioned my aptitude to really do this. The fall hunts on the other hand would be on the salmon streams and much less arduous. After much ado and consternation I finally concluded that it might be foolish to spend that kind of money and go down to an area and not be able to do the climbing that might be entailed. In the springtime the bears are often up on the snow line although they work their way down to the creeks as the season progresses. Fortunately, the deposit was dutifully returned and I again scratched my head as to what I should do or not do. I had often thought about returning to Kamchatka Peninsula but the airline situation had deteriorated almost completely and I hoped something might come available but this was not the case. The alternative is going halfway around the world through New York City and on to Moscow and then entire far east of Russia. I did find an outfit that had the concession for twenty years and the owner was highly regarded and interestingly, they had lived in Wisconsin in an area that I was very familiar with. I did speak with the owner who enthusiastically assured me that those taking over the concession would still have the same Russian camps and guides, which is critical of course in this kind of outing. Also, he said that some of his intermediate help was available that knew all the ins and outs of the customs and transportation issues that turned out to be extremely helpful. Nonetheless, the trip was very daunting in terms of the logistics and I have an aversion to major airports and the confusion and all that goes with that, particularly when you take a firearm internationally you can expect to have great problems of some sort. This, as it turned out, was the case. My oldest son Timothy was more than generous in securing me a business class ticket, having extensive experience in international travel and he knew the downside of eight and ten hour flights, time changes involved, etc.. This certainly was a far cry from being back in the dungeon of third class coach. I tried to become as well-versed as possible on all of the potential snafus that might occur and did speak to two gentlemen that had been on the trip previously, both of which were up in age and the one fellow did say that upon his return he did have a heart reaction that he was still dealing with. He did give me some pointers that came in very handing including that the ammunition was to be in a locked case and separate from the firearm although in other places the ammunition has to be in the closed firearm case, etc. so we situation has to be carefully explored. My wife Judy had accompanied me to our son's home in Springfield , MA and after visiting some, we made our way to the airport in New York City. I truly appreciated their support as fumbling through that airport with all my gear was more than I could deal with. Sure enough when we arrived, one or two other fellows were already being hung up on a technicality, namely they did not have locks on their ammunition cases and had to run out via taxis to find a lock box and barely made it back in time for a departure.

From there it was miles and miles of flight time and I think in total it was twelve different time zones, all of which left you zombified and rummy to say the least. We were told that an interpreter would be available in the Moscow airport and would help us get through the maze of inspections. I asked the outfitter how would I know this particular person as the airport is huge and he said just look for the prettiest girl that you've ever seen. Sure enough, this was the case as we arrived in the baggage area a strikingly beautiful lady was there with a trench coat and looked like something out of Vogue magazine. Here name was Galina and despite her appearance she was the most friendly and down to earth gal that one would want to have. Fortunately she also had the expertise and experience to provide assistance, which was crucial in this circumstance. She was good enough to trek us around Moscow and down into the bowels of underground railroad, which I'm sure during World War II was a bomb shelter. I swear it was at least fifty or seventy five feet down. After getting off that airplane then starting walking was a bit of a challenge for me as the other two gentlemen that accompanied me were a good deal younger. She took us down to the famous Red Square and St. Basil Russian Orthodox church and of course she knew all of the fine dining places that were in the area. I remember the cost of the meal was several hundreds of dollars, which one of the gentlemen picked up and both of them were successful business owners so I didn't feel terribly bad at accepting their generous offering. The hotel was connected to the airport, however, one still had to leave security which created a whole scenario of having gear checked and again, the firearm was always a problem and had to be individually handled through their airport police. The next morning found us up early and having to go through the TSA process and this is where the most significant happening that occurred and it was not a happy situation for sure. One rather angry looking Russian woman who was managing the x-ray machine kept running my gear through the conveyor belt over and over again and finally she started pointing in a very vigorous way and called me over to show me what she was perseverating about. Low and behold in one of my gloves was a small caliber bullet that in their eyes was a major problem. She was quickly on the telephone and before long three sets of KGB type plain clothes people showed and the merry-go-round began in earnest. There were extraordinary amounts of communicating and arm waving and it became more grave as more people showed up and it was as if I had violated the most sacred of all rules. Galina throughout was very calm and kept telling me that his was serious in their eyes but that she would persevere through it and this turned out to be the case. She was pacing continuously and was on the telephone speaking to, I suspect, her contacts. Fortunately, as it turned out, her father was in the Russian Air Force as a pilot and her boyfriend was in some special-ops and I believe that he was instrumental in breaking loose this quagmire of bureaucracy. After much ado the next thing I knew I was being escorted down to the basement jail area and more deliberations, all of which I was not privy to but I found myself being photographed twice with fingerprints and then the signing of a multitude of papers began, all of which would have been extraordinarily intimidating if I did not have the resource of Galina who kept telling me which and where to sign on the documents and she obviously was able to discern what I was not signing my life away. After about three hours of this, somebody gave the go-ahead and we were able to find our way back up the stairs almost at the time the flight was leaving. The flight from Moscow to Petropavlovsk occurs only once a day and the bookings are solid so missing this flight would have resulted in a total disaster for the hunt. As we rushed to the boarding gate I compounded the embarrassment by catching my knee brace on a chair, which sent me sprawling face first amidst the ongoers and then humbly picking up my body and gear once again. Fortunately, I didn't break anything although I hit hard on my right shoulder and head. After the debacle in Moscow, the trip went relatively smooth although again, we looked at another ten or twelve hours of flight time across eastern Russia and into Petropavlovsk early in the morning where we faced another rigorous go-around regarding the firearm inspection but certainly nothing like the one in Moscow. In my previous trips to Russia we had smooth sailing as we were able to fly directly to Petro and the airport at that point was very small and customs was a relatively simple process and the return was even better as we could take the hide in a duffle bag and throw it into the baggage area with minimal expense. Arriving in Anchorage was also easy as the customs people were there to meet the airplane and would expeditiously go through the import/export process.

Landing in Petro was a bit of a flash back as I had been there two previous times but I could see that things had gotten a little more sophisticated then when I first went there. The airport was larger and the baggage process was a little more involved than my previous experiences.

Sure enough, two of the young guides who where very athletic looking fellows where there to grab our gear and the next thing we knew we were down the road in a Toyota type of SUV although our heads were still swirling from the extended time of our travels. We were on our way to the far southern coast of Kamchatka, literally across from the Bering Sea that would have brought us to Alaska. The trip down a rather bumping muddy road was at least five hours long and not terribly pleasant but we were happy to have arrived. Once we reached the coast arrived at a very small disheveled looking town and the bleakness of the area is very apparent. Everything is made of concrete and looks like a military post of some sort and not a very comfortable environment. One can clearly see that the economy of Russia is indeed in bad shape as is reflected in their maintenance of their roads and the conditions of their buildings, etc.. The next thing we knew we had to dive through our duffle bags pulling out gear that we would need as we had to take a small boat across a sizeable stretch of water to the main camp so it was a struggle to redress and repack all your gear after the long air trip. The next thing we knew we were bouncing across the waves in an eighteen foot type of runabout and it wasn't the best of days as it was raining and very reminiscent of my time on the ocean in Valdez. I would guess that after several hours we found our way to the camp and we were greeted by a very friendly camp group including the father of one of the guides that was handling the boat and also another interpreter and camp cook. So began our ventures that started early the next morning. My travel partner was a fellow named Max who was from, I believe, Virginia and had in fact never seen a bear. I was trying to give him some pointers on what to look for in terms of size, etc.. For the outfitters he was a great find as they would not have to show him much in that he was keen to take any kind of bear that presented itself. Sure enough, the next morning they already had him on a relatively nice bear and he was quite tickled with the outcome. The bear was only a few miles down from where the camp was and he said he had to do some running to get in position but all in all he was done in several hours which then left me as the lone man out and I knew this was gonna turn into a down and dirty, persuasive matter as I had experienced before, that if you're the last man out they want to get you a bear and get you out so they can close up camp for the winter. This in fact was the last group to come into the camp and I had picked it specifically as I was concerned about the quality of hair and it was the first week of October, which puts it at a very marginal level. I know that they take bears in late August and September but having much experience with bear hides I knew at that point that the hair would be very marginal and not worthwhile as often the roots would slip and the hair would come out.

I began my outing early the next morning with the use

of an Argo, which is an amphibious ATV type of machine that has been around for some time and are quite expensive. I went with the big boss who was the Godfather of the camp, a very kind and friendly sort. He also obviously had the most experience of all of the guides, which I think were only two. We took off through some God-awful trails that I'm more than familiar with the bouncing and being shook from side to side as we went through deep ruts and mud and swampy type of area, although when we did get out to the flats it was again very familiar as Alaska is covered with this type of tundra, particularly around the ocean where the tidal flats create a myriad of creeks, all of which support salmon runs and of course this is what the bears spend their time doing as they move from creek to creek looking for easy pickings. I felt very much at home as I had spent God knows how many days in this terrain over the years in Alaska and it rekindled a lot of feelings from previous ventures. In fact, Valdez itself is surrounded by pretty extensive tidal flats that I passed by every day in my forty years in Alaska. We did finally spot at least one bear that we sat down and glassed for some time and then finally positioned ourselves in a way in which we got in front of the bear and let him move in our direction. He was probably in the seven to eight foot range, none of which I was interested in but a very pretty critter for sure. We also did another neat stalk with the Argo because again the tundra is hard to walk on because it's full of hummocks and slush but we did get very close to this bear and he was a much better trophy but we decided was way too early to make a decision and I certainly wasn't in the business of taking the first bear that I had seen.

By this time it was in the afternoon and the sun was setting some and we started our way back towards the camp and at some point Sergei all of a sudden had a bolt of enthusiasm and the speed of the Argo increased appreciably and I could see that something had spurred his interest. They do carry two-way radios and I'm ascertaining that his son has spotted something worth our effort. We went crashing through eight-foot tall alders and he was hell bent on getting to where we were going in a very fast time. At one point he jumped off of his Argo with an ax in hand and within moments he had cut down and approximately eight-foot tall limb that had a fork in the end and he obviously had chopped a lot of wood as each stroke was done so efficiently. He strapped that onto the Argo and off we went until we reached a sizeable splinter of the main river that had a sharp bank down and I could see he was looking carefully for a way out of it once we got into the water and then trying to get up on the other bank. He picked a bank but as it turned out it was way too steep for getting up and we found ourselves almost up on end with me in the back and God knows if the Argo would have tipped over I would have been in a world of shit. As it turned out he was able to find his way out of the Argo and fortunately had a wench on the Argo and then I could see why he had cut out this big limb. He proceeded to force it into the mud at a very sharp angle then put his arm through the fork and then wrapped the end of the wench to the bottom of the limb and the only help I was that I could stretch out and push the wench button forward which succeeded in us extracting the machine off of the bank. From there we headed across an island of sorts as I think there was water on both sides and we went back and forth, back and forth and he was obviously looking for something his son had spotted.

The next morning found us at breakfast, which was quite good, and also with a renewed sense of enthusiasm. One of the boys had been up early in the morning and apparently had a lookout point high above the camp where they could over look the tundra flats and had seen that same bear that they were interested in the night before. Thus we were encouraged to move quickly and down the hill we found ourselves in a small skiff that I previously described and made our way down to the stream that they had seen the bear fishing from and/or wandering the bank. We quietly floated the creek which was actually more of a small river and this went on for not terribly long when I looked up and to my amazement I was staring at a bears head that was only, I'm guessing, ten or fifteen feet away from the boat and he was laying down either eating a fish or resting. Usually I am quick on the draw but somehow I was fumbling that morning and didn't respond as quickly as I should have and then everything broke into a flurry of activity that still remains a blur. The bear obviously sensed our presence and turned and took off running, in the meantime the guide who was just a young fella was yelling at me to get up on the bow of the boat which involved climbing over the windshield which was no easy task given my lumbering condition and he grabbed me by the arm and I somehow pulled my way over the top and onto a slippery small bow area. All I could see is the bear as he was galloping through the five-foot tall grass. In other instances I would have never taken a shot but he encouraged me to shoot and I still don't know how that all transpired as he shot quickly after with a military style AK-47. In any event, the bear went down and we were elated at the moment because in other instances the bear would have gotten away in that thick cover. Usually you do not take a running shot at a brown bear unless of course it's wounded and you usually want the time to size it up and really make an informed decision that this is what you

were after. I felt in some ways that I was getting the bum's rush into taking this bear without really having a chance to confirm my interest.

After fumbling off the boat we made our way close to the bear and by then the big boss Sergei was arriving with two dogs that surrounded the bear that was still very much alive but you could see was down for the count. I did not want to shoot at the bear as both of his dogs were very close to the front of it and I didn't want to take a chance that the bullet could go through the critter and into one of his dogs so I worked my way around to the back of the bear where I could take a back shot that would hopefully sever the spine and sure enough he was down for good within seconds. So there we were with a wet bear that looked good but not great and pictures, etc. were taken and I was still kind of shaking my head about the circumstances as I often second-guess the things that I do but did feel I was getting a bit of a bum's rush.

Several other staff finally got down to the bear and they were quick to get the hide off after the picture taking and we went back to camp. They had previously been worrying about a big storm that was supposed to arrive that afternoon and we were seeing the beginnings of that and that was a partial explanation why we were in such a rush for this bear as the storm they thought, might stay on for a few days we would just be sitting in the cabins which was obviously something they did not want to do. Hunting in rain is fine but blowing rain is beyond the pale. The next day found us truly in a full-blown storm and the wind was blowing and I was going to give them assistance in the final skinning but they were doing it under a tarp and there was not much room for my help although I thought they were doing a relatively decent job. The preliminary measurements were ten feet from claw to claw in the front and somewhere close to nine feet from nose to tail. The most impressive measurements were the circumference of the bear at seventy-four inches around the chest and eighty-four around the belly so it quite a chunky critter but they do describe the Siberian bears as being a different body style than the Alaskan bears and refer to them as being quadratic which is more square-like in their anatomy. The following day or so was spent in the rainy but comfortable cabin and then after several days of that we had a moment where Sergei felt it was clear enough to make the trek back to the mainland and it was obvious you did not want to get into the swells with the small craft that we were operating so finally we decided that it was time to go before we got further hung up at the cabin and away we went across a pretty extensive piece of water that would have been dangerous in other more turbulent conditions.

Upon our arrival at the dock we again had to demobilize all of our gear and off we went to the lodging which was actually a very nice hotel but unfortunately it was twenty miles from the main town which was not my liking as we basically all had nothing to do but sit at the lodge type hotel since we were so far away from the local culture. We did make one trip into town but I would have preferred to stay in a less luxurious type of hotel and be more of a part of the local culture instead. We did have the luxury of a hot water bath that I think was part of the volcanic underground that surrounded the area and so that was quite a nice reprieve but the three or four days we spent at the hotel was not worthwhile and I again was looking forward to wandering the streets of Petro and looking at the local scenery and people. We did make a little tour of the area and sure enough did spot a Russian submarine that was escorted by two destroyer type of ships and as noted previously, this part of Siberia was off limits to everybody for many years as it was their hub of both aircraft and submarine activity that were very much kept secret to even the locals.

The return home went much more smoothly with no major snafus except for the less than helpful people at the New York airport where I had to transfer my gear from one concourse to another and it took a bit of cajoling and money to get someone to help drag my gear up through to the domestic flights.

As I reflect back on the trip I don't know if it was worthwhile. It certainly was more expensive than I thought and particularly when we got the extraordinary bill for the importation of the hide through several countries that was not given to us ahead of time. The bear is currently in the process of being put together and I was going to do it myself but really didn't have the space to work on it nor the physicality of stretching that hide as I have done a number of bears before and know how much work is involved. Hopefully it will come out in a fine manner and I will probably bequeath it to my son if he is interested but will sit and admire it for a few years until that time. So ends the wild and wooly trips abroad. I can't imagine that I would ever be able to take another nor would I be interested. I will stick to my bird hunting with my little dog, Fergie, and make a few trips to Canada that I'm very comfortable with and always have a good time.

Precious with mounted bear

Appendix

This will serve as a disclaimer for all of the previous verbiage. It was recited verbatim "off the cuff" with 'nary' a written word. I guess it is a testament to my recollection of these many tales. I hope they are correct as I was hoping to recall the details before I slip into dementia as has affected so many of our illustrious leaders. Dare I say more.